The Eradication of
By Social M

The Eradication of Humanity
By Social Media

*Disclaimer: All information in this book is accurate at the
time of this writing. Under the Fair Use Law, everything
mentioned is for informational purposes only and should not
be used against anyone.*

The Eradication of Humanity
By Social Media

The Eradication of Humanity
By Social Media

The Eradication of Humanity
By Social Media

The Eradication of Humanity
By Social Media

The Eradication of Humanity
By Social Media

The Eradication of Humanity
By Social Media

Table of Contents

The Eradication of Humanity
By Social Media

The Eradication of Humanity
By Social Media

The Eradication of Humanity
By Social Media

Chapter One

The Corrupt World of Social Media

*The Internet and social media are manipulative and may one
day destroy us all.*

The Eradication of Humanity
By Social Media

Welcome to the dark world of TikTok, the popular video app that has taken over the world of 2021 like a raging, angry storm. This ever-demanding platform is all about who can become the next big "thing," who has the most talent, who is the most popular, and who has the largest clout . . . at least, that's what it wants us to believe.

Like all trending social media platforms, TikTok is yet another app people can use to show off the wealth they don't have and their self-proclaimed fame, from videos of luxuries that don't belong to them to paparazzi and fans that aren't actually following them—all just to achieve that highly-coveted fame. We all want to be TikTok famous like we all wanted to be YouTube famous or Instagram famous; it's all just another platform for desperate people to try to achieve a celebrity status with the most minimal effort possible.

Among Facebook, Snapchat, Instagram, and Twitter, TikTok has become the newest social media platform that grazes everyone's lips, and we all want to be part of this new trend, whatever it takes. Like cliques in high school, we all want to be the popular ones and have our faces plastered all over the Internet so people will recognize us wherever we go and worship us with gifts and love.

We all crave that verified checkmark next to our names, and we thrive on the chance to be sponsored because that means we finally "made it."

We all want to be influencers despite knowing that we don't have any talent, using our filters and our bodies to achieve the same fame people have spent their entire lives trying to achieve.

Social media has turned our egos against us, making us believe that we deserve to be showered with free compliments, presents, and vacations just because we're famous online.

The Eradication of Humanity
By Social Media

Reality check—nobody cares!

We've become desperate to do whatever we can to achieve the status of a public figure or Internet personality. And with TikTok's feature of showing the total *like* counts our profiles receive, we strive to do whatever we can in order to become sponsored and get paid. We cook, dance, sing, hurt ourselves, and turn ourselves into fools just so others will notice us and pay us the slightest of attention that we always wished we had from our parents.

We even go as far as to take the lives of innocent people around us just so we can chase clout, destroying our humanity and turning us into monsters.

Oh, what had gone so tragically wrong in our lives that we yearn so much for strangers' attention?

Becoming Internet famous is getting out of hand, with people rising to fame just as quickly as others are getting cancelled for their impulsive and frantic attempts to maintain status even after they have run out of content to post. And TikTok is the single greatest platform of our generation, where achieving recognition with minimal effort is possible. We all know it, and many of us try to develop creative ways day after day to achieve this dream. We resort to putting down others just to boost ourselves up, trash-talking our competitors so we can steal their fans, and even risking other's lives.

Remind you of any other social media platform?

Like all of them?

We live in a world where we no longer have to or want to work for anything, letting the idea of "quick and easy fame" obstruct our minds. We all expect people to hand us free things, things they have spent hundreds of hours making or tons of money purchasing, just because we think we're famous and deserve them. Having 10 million followers on social media for doing absolutely nothing doesn't make us famous; it makes us hungry for attention and displays how desperate we actually are.

We live in a world where it has become acceptable to sit around AND still see the cash roll in. This trend makes us all become lazy, unmotivated to go out and make an honest, sustainable living.

What happened to the days where we had to work hard to achieve our goals?

Do we even have goals and dreams anymore?

Or are we just frantically trying out different hobbies to find one that will finally make it big on the Internet?

Is there anything we won't film and post?

Have our lives all become so public that if we don't provide proof of the things we do, then they never actually happened?

TikTok was expected to take over the social media world when it was founded by ByteDance in 2016. And that it did. By exploiting the gap left in the market by the former application, Musical.ly, TikTok gave users what they wanted. As a result, many became hooked on this platform, from its user-friendly uploads to fun and creative filters, long before most of us even knew of its existence.

In comparison to other platforms, TikTok is still relatively new. Facebook was born in 2004 as the brainchild of Harvard students wanting to connect with classmates. Today, it's a multibillion-dollar company boasting 2.8 billion active users across the globe. Though older, the social media giant still has its claws deep in the market. Facebook is successful because it uses FOMO, or the fear of missing out, to keep us addicted. If all of our friends and family are posting photographs or life updates online, we don't want to feel left out.

Shortly after, YouTube went live in 2005. Now, 31 million YouTube channels exist, and 5 billion videos get watched every single day. Another mindboggling fact? It's also the second most visited website in the world.

But if we want to talk more current stats, let's look at Instagram. Originally created in 2010, Instagram, or the 'gram, was advertised as a sleeker, more millennial-friendly option for mobile phone users. The app has since exploded in popularity. More than 50 billion photos have been uploaded, ranging from pictures of breakfast pancakes to travel destinations to cats wearing hats. If you want to see it, chances are, it's on there. Instagram is also notoriously known for its fake portrayal of destinations and the human body, with attractive feeds and nudity outperforming other content.

Then there's Twitch. Once widely known for video game streaming, it has now expanded to broader horizons and opportunities. Another relatively new contender, Twitch crashed through the social media glass ceiling in 2011. Founded by Justin Kan, it reels people in as a way to not only watch live gaming streams, but ASMR, music, art, and fashion as well. In 2020, 3.8 million content creators used Twitch to get their messages and stories out. Since Amazon bought it, the numbers just keep growing.

To say that social media revolutionized our lives would be an understatement. In less than two decades, humanity went through a social media tsunami. By its very nature, social media is constantly changing. Only the best will stick around long enough to succeed. Our first case study: TikTok

The main reason TikTok became such a huge success is that it was a new addition to the already existing market that allowed its users to share, like, and comment on visually appealing content made by others and themselves. Creators can post short clips that either showcase their "unique" talents or flex their lives to others on the Internet as a way of exerting their dominance and status. This type of content makes others drool over influencers—content that people watch like pornography because it gives them a second-hand experience of having things they know they can never achieve. It simply acts as bait for others to browse through their content in hopes of becoming viral.

Not everything we see on the Internet is true. People who claim to own ten cars can just be filming a random person's driveway. People who claim to have millions in cash could have just printed wads of fake money to flex their lack of wealth. Like on all social media, we all want to become TikTok influencers, something that seems unachievable. Still, all we need is one viral video that takes us from the bottom to the top...just like all it takes is one video to bring us from top to bottom.

Chapter Two

When Society Began to Fall Apart

With over 800 million active followers that continue to grow each day, TikTok has become especially popular among the younger crowds. These young adults use the app to record every moment of their everyday lives, from the moment they wake up—including what they eat to where they shop—to the moment they go to bed, their entire lives plastered all over the Internet.

Nothing is private anymore.

We willingly expose all the discretions of our existence for just a few minutes of fame, if any.

TikTok targets mainly the younger generation, those between the ages of 16 and 24, as their feeble minds are vulnerable enough to fall for the false hope of fame that social media platforms claim to provide. Those who have never had to truly work for their way of life are those who dream big, believing the world will hand them anything for a flash of a smile. They believe that money and success come to those who are most attractive or owns the most name-brand things.

While this is true to an extent, it's this same mentality that ruins the future of this generation as they chase after a dream they can never obtain, wasting their best years on the Internet rather than living up to their potentials.

This generation, or Generation Z, accounts for more than 17 billion views on TikTok PER MONTH, as well as over two billion downloads worldwide, with a rising increase in its aggressive growth. TikTok surfaced in the middle of an ever-changing digital age as a new contestant, facing giants like Facebook and Instagram. While they remain relevant, they have been overshadowed by the rising influence of the video app. Adding the Chinese wallet to its growing popularity, they are left with an extensively ambitious app ready to take over the world.

Moreover, TikTok came to power at a time when social media had already become both an addiction and a social way to prove one's existence, a chance for users to shout to the world that they matter.

The Eradication of Humanity
By Social Media

Ask anyone born before the year 2000 what social media was like, and you'll find that they struggle to give a precise answer. That's because, until early into the twenty-first century, there weren't a lot of options out there. Sure, AOL Instant Messenger was around. Blogging was just beginning to catch on. But for the most part, social media wasn't at the forefront of anyone's mind.

Our identities weren't tied to a digital platform. We didn't rely on influencers to tell us what products to buy. A phone was, well...just a phone; a hashtag was just known as the "pound key."

Along came Facebook. Suddenly, everybody is signing up for an account, from the average Joe all the way up to presidents and world leaders. For the first time, we could yell into the void and get a reply back. And not just during the day. Facebook was a 24/7 space to share every moment of our lives and feel that our presence was significant enough to spend hours upon hours documenting and videotaping. Facebook may have been the spark that started the burning fire of what social media has become.

As the figures keep rising, it has become a concerning fact that people are growing dependent on the Internet, unable to live for themselves without constantly relying on others to validate them or tell them right from wrong and the beliefs they should abide by. We are already living in a world where we only take action after someone else already has, following trends rather than leading them.

When TikTok came swooping in on the trending wave, it took advantage of the opportunity to propel off the charts, taking the place that Vine blatantly left open in 2015 after it dismantled and disappeared. Its existence was too obsolete to compete with the giants of Snapchat and Instagram. Because Vine also refused to monetize the content of its users for financial benefit, many once-loyal users began to abandon the app, leaving it high and dry. At the same time that Vine was struggling to keep afloat, Musical.ly was launched and quickly rose to the status of the only video-based social media network, with approximately 160 million users.

When TikTok bought the promising platform and became the sole replacement in the growing industry, it secured for itself a bright future and promising development. However, many believed that the video app was created from mystery, with a dark past, finding the death of the co-founder of Vine oddly suspicious shortly after TikTok sprung into the market. What really happened? No one knows since they simply brushed it off as an overdose, a diagnosis that seemed close to unbelievable.

Was this a coincidence? Or did the two incidences fit too well together, almost as if they were staged? To this day, many still believe that the two occurrences were somehow related, but whether this was a conspiracy theory or a disguised truth is difficult to say.

What is TikTok all about? Why and how did it become so popular so suddenly, rising up the social chain with other popular platforms? How did it stand out against many others as an app to be reckoned with? Simple. TikTok took the video aspects that people all know and love from other apps and channeled them into one large platform, allowing users worldwide to animate their personal lives and create meaningful and relatable content in the eyes of the consumers.

The use of short video clips that grasp the eyes of those with short attention spans makes going viral that much easier, with the majority of people using TikTok to portray their minimal to zero skills and tweaking them with filters for others to admire. Not only that, its liberty to host any kind of content—from cooking to singing to drawing—has gained a lot of attention.

The Eradication of Humanity
By Social Media

We're all looking for ways to distract ourselves from the woes of life, distractions that don't consume much of our time, distractions we can scroll through and watch within a matter of seconds.

This very fact allowed the creators of TikTok to create a platform that became a huge success, targeting the short attention spans of people as they scroll through their phones in class, at work, or on the toilet, ultimately becoming their main selling point. Also, as the app is versatile and available worldwide, people can connect with each other from all over the globe, something that can't be said for apps like Instagram, banned in the very same country that created the video app. A coincidence? Or just a witty marketing scheme to dominate the social media world?

While the content and topics on TikTok cater to many different age groups, the most popular is limited to challenges and dance routines that attract children and teenagers looking for easy, quick fun. They see this content online and seek to recreate the trends or start their own. It's the lazy person's way into getting likes online without much effort other than doing in front of a camera what they would typically do in the privacies of their own bedrooms, with and without clothing.

We also live in a world where the current generation shames the ones preceding it for being "too old" to use TikTok, acting like they own the platform and taking the privilege away from parents and older generations. TikTok is notoriously known as THE APP for GenZ, much like Instagram was known as the app for millennials. Nowadays, if we're not trending on TikTok, then we might as well be a nobody.

Social media is enticing because there is something for everyone. Like a drug of choice, each person can find a specific niche for their specific taste. GenZ may cringe at Facebook, but that's only because the average age of the typical user in the United

The Eradication of Humanity
By Social Media

States is 40 years old. In contrast, older generations scoff at live-streaming platforms like Twitch.

"Who in their right mind would rather watch somebody else play a video game than play it themselves?" they wonder.

The answer here doesn't matter. What's important is how social media preys upon our need for socialization and then presents us with the "perfect" solution. It's like a buffet. You pick what you like, and I'll get what I like. Before we know it, we're all so gorged on social media that we don't even think twice about why.

Like many other social media platforms, such as Instagram and YouTube, TikTok offers the chance for creators to monetize their work and create brands and trends, which brings even more hopefuls searching for an easy way to make money and gain fame. Top celebrities and influencers quickly jumped on board to increase their recognition, especially during the confinement period that COVID-19 created, generating new ways to entertain the crowds and fans that didn't require traveling or public dining.

Celebrities like Will Smith quickly rose to 38 million followers on TikTok, with Jason Derulo not far behind. Bonding with their fans over their shared presence and humor, they both topped the charts as two of the top ten most followed TikTok creators at the time of this writing.

However, they don't even come close to the top of the list. 16-year-old dancer, Charli D'Amelio, rose to fame for her dance performances that gained the attention of over 111 million followers and 9 billion likes, earning her a net worth of 8 million dollars and counting!

How did one young girl go from being an average person to having so much fame and notoriety so quickly?

The Eradication of Humanity
By Social Media

How did a bunch of videos of someone merely dancing become so popular and attractive?

What drives people to like one video over another?

Do social viewers prefer content that makes them envious of the creators, or do they prefer relatable content?

The algorithm for Internet success remains unknown.

Of course, celebrities who have a preexisting fan base will find it easier to make it big on TikTok. When they create an account, fans follow them over from whatever other social media app they were already connected to. Maybe one of the most well-known is Kylie Jenner. She was a celebrity in her own right when she joined TikTok, but for her, the app opened a whole new global crowd of young eyes hungry for her vanity posts.

At 28.4 million followers, people flock to her page for content about makeup, workout routines, and to get a glimpse of the rich and famous lifestyle. Whether it's the latest lipstick, swimming in the crystal blue waters of some tropical island paradise, or promoting her line of cosmetics, Kylie is an expert at showing us how she is living the dream...even if she isn't. Hey, if we can't attain the fame ourselves, at least we can live vicariously through her, right?

The concept of "going viral" is what drives ordinary people to aim for fame. Like D'Amelio and Jenner, many others quickly rose to TikTok stardom. Take Celina Myers (who goes by @celinaspookyboo), for example. She was an average girl from a small town in southwestern Ontario, Canada, who started her TikTok account recently in 2019. Since then, her popularity has exploded. In the beginning, the average views on each of her videos were about 4,000. Not bad, but not great.

Today, she has 15.5 million followers and 439.5 million likes. How'd she do it? By posting comical – often self-deprecating –

videos that made fun of herself pretending to sleepwalk. If there's one thing TikTok fans crave, it's watching others embarrass themselves for their own personal amusement. By giving us a glimpse into her private life, inviting us into her room, Celina has gone from being a little-known creator to having a net worth of $700,000. Not too shabby considering all she does is bang into furniture.

The list goes on and on and on. Another seemingly normal guy who made it big is Brody Wellmaker. His bio states, "Future Oscar-Winning Actor." It seems his 8.7 million followers would agree. His views soared on TikTok after posting a video of himself acting like characters in the Twilight films. The clip went viral! Fans literally begged for more. Kristen Stewart impersonations was a trend on fire. Not long after, that coveted blue checkmark magically appeared next to his name. As they say, the rest is history.

Another piece of TikTok's popularity is the reliance on well-known mainstream media songs implemented into the app that users can base their content around. Creators use songs they love for backup music and montages, allowing them to drive attention and generate flow from mediocre content.

These songs also help promote trends, such as Mia Khalifa's Hit or Miss or Cardi B's WAP, where people attempt to recreate these viral dances for fame.

Following that stage, new users can also discover different music outside of their general repertoire, giving small artists and indie musicians a chance for their music to become renowned. As a result, more and more began to create and perform their own pieces, pairing them with trendy dance moves or memes so others would notice them.

TikTok also plays to the broader audience with shorter attention spans, with video clips cut into 15-60 second pieces that are easy to focus on and catch onto people's minds. Shorter videos are more likely to go viral than longer ones that lose people as our attentions are short-lived, and we can't focus on one thing for too long. This hack gives creators a higher chance of possible Internet careers as they continue to discover their niche. Short music clips also give independent artists the chance to sign with producers, an opportunity they would've struggled to get otherwise.

Needless to say, this app is single-handedly turning ordinary people into celebrities.

Chapter Three

How Far Will We Go for Clout?

Although TikTok stands out as a video-based platform, it doesn't differ much from other existing social platforms. While it's true that Facebook mainly revolves around staying in touch with lost connections, Twitter revolves around short, curt messages and quotes with confusing AF hashtags to grab the attention of others, and Instagram is all about who has the most talent when it comes to Photoshopping and fake followers, they all boil down to providing people with one thing: clout. In the grand scheme of things, TikTok is simply another form of social media created to brainwash people and steal their personal information, with a sense of false hope for fame in return.

Like many other platforms before, TikTok's objective is to keep people scrolling through the endless "For You Page" they are most known for to get users hooked on their content. Most of us don't want to admit it, but we spend an average of 52 minutes a day on TikTok, opening the app at least 8 times a day, with those between the ages of 4 and 15 spending at least 80 minutes daily on this app.

Why are 4-year-olds even on TikTok?

Why are people on the Internet getting younger and younger?

Why is 8-year-old Milana Makhanets married to 13-year-old Pasha Pai?

Are they even old enough to know what the concept of marriage is?

Children should be spending their time outside, enjoying life, not staring nonstop at a phone screen.

Let's investigate video-based social media for a moment. First of all, it's passive. Unlike sports or hobbies, platforms such as TikTok, YouTube, and Twitch require very little of us. To participate, we simply click "play." The entrance fee is zero, and so is the effort. But remember, nothing is truly free. In exchange for entertainment, we trade our attention as well as our most valuable asset – time. Time is the one thing in this world we cannot get back. That's what makes it so precious to social media companies. They know this, and they purposely

The Eradication of Humanity
By Social Media

make it easy for us to forget about the clock. Features such as automatically playing the next video (looking at you, YouTube!) or endless scrolling options (hey, Instagram!) kill our productivity. Sure, it's fun. But think about the amount of time we lose forever, glued to a screen.

Creators on TikTok do whatever they can to develop content that will get users to spend hours and hours a day on their pages. The more traffic and views they receive, the higher their chances are of becoming TikTok famous and sponsored. While most of us average users spend about a minute altogether filming and posting, those hungry for fame and attention spend hours a day coming up with the PERFECT idea for their videos and researching the type of content that will generate the most traffic and likes—including murdering their loved ones and neighbors on camera to become popular.

Yes, you read that correctly. People will literally *kill* for a few minutes of TikTok fame. Take, for instance, the case of Zachary Latham. After a series of ongoing disputes over noise and reckless driving with his neighbor in South Jersey, eighteen-year-old Zachary decided it would be a good idea to start recording his encounters and posting them online. Tragically, one particular argument went too far. Following a heated fight, Zachary stabbed his neighbor, William Durham. The man was pronounced dead at the hospital.

Some might say this was just a dispute that got out of hand. Or perhaps it was self-defense. But why then, did Latham film the whole thing? And why film it when several other witnesses were standing by watching the event unfold? The answer is simple. He was obsessed with going viral on TikTok. Prosecutors working on the case claimed that he intended to "lure the Durhams there, attack them, and record it for TikTok."

Another example is the case of the Christchurch Mosque Shootings, where madman Brenton Tarrant killed 51 people. With an intent on murdering Muslims, Tarrant went on a shooting rampage that he live-streamed for 17 minutes on Facebook. Why? To spread his message of hate on a popular social media platform for all to see.

Live-streamed crime doesn't stop there, sadly. In 2019, German neo-Nazi, Stephan Balliet, used Twitch to record himself shooting at a German synagogue and Turkish kebab shop. He murdered two people. Again, live-streamed for attention.

Much more recently, in 2021, YouTube became an oblivious host to the streaming of a shooting. Ten innocent lives were taken in Boulder, Colorado when Ahmad Al Aliwi Alissa ran inside a grocery store with a gun. Part of the attack was live-streamed by a bystander. Unfortunately, those documented make up only a few. Countless more violent crimes go unreported all the time.

Murderers, or at the very least, those with pending homicide charges, are like celebrities on TikTok, Facebook, and YouTube. The scarier the content they post, the more we gobble it up. As a result, one of the highest-rated content types includes young girls dancing like strip club entertainers on the platform. This type of content attracts pedophiles and sleazy people on the Internet with fetishes for watching young UNDERAGED girls flaunt their bodies in sexualized manners. Despite how great the algorithm is in promoting similar videos of interest for people to watch on TikTok, it cannot judge whether or not that content is appropriate. This results in showing half-naked bodies and hypersexualized videos of young preteens to men in their 40s.

And since users are not forced to reveal their age or gender, the TikTok algorithm has no way of realizing how sickening it is for a fifty-year-old man to watch videos of thirteen-year-old girls dancing or playing (on a loop). It will keep providing him with similar videos, not knowing the possible ill-intentions of the person behind the screen. Pedophilic thoughts are nothing but an example of the potential harm this algorithm can bring.

The Eradication of Humanity
By Social Media

But TikTok isn't the only guilty party. The media has roasted Twitch because of the platform's inability to curb misogyny, sexism, and the hyper-sexualization of female streamers. In a New York Times article published in 2020, dozens of streamers came forward to talk about their experiences with being the victims of disgusting comments and body-shaming slander. Internet creators never know who might be watching, if they're capturing screenshots/filming, or what their end goals are. When we put our private lives out in public, our actions are there for all to see. The attention we get could be positive, reinforcing our thoughts about ourselves. But it can also be bad. Sexism, racism, slander…it's all on the table for a live streamer.

Ironically, female streamers often intentionally use their bodies to sexualize themselves and get rewarded with more viewers on platforms. Visually presenting ourselves in a targeted way that pleases our audience is a proven method for gaining fans fast. Streaming in a bikini or other revealing clothing has been proven to generate more traffic than filming in sweats and a t-shirt. So, the circle continues on and on and on.

But on the flip side, male streamers have complained that Twitch is sexist against *them*! In a Reddit chat discussion, anonymous posters claimed that while Twitch is lenient towards female streamers being hypersexual, it often disciplines or outright bans male streamers for sharing similar content. Basically, partial nudity is okay if you're a girl. Boys, sorry, you are shit out of luck.

The argument is that the algorithm is sexist, and this is problematic because the chance to earn money is higher if you are one gender over the other. Haven't you ever noticed that when couples have separate channels or pages, the girls always have three times as many worshippers?

It's a damned if you do, damned if you don't situation. Stream hypersexual content, and you're a target of disgusting comments. Don't, and the audience finds somebody else who will pander to their fantasies. Either way, Twitch is making money.

Again, this only proves that the ways social media encourage us to use our bodies for attention are subject to questionable algorithm programming. Intended or not, there are bound to be consequences.

On a different note, all these videos are not necessarily as organized as we expect them to be. They don't obey any chronological timeline. Many users lure and trap their viewers by creating content with cliffhanger endings or click-bait titles, with thrilling stories expanded to last several videos. Many are controversial, while others are just plain dumb.

Ron White wasn't lying when he said, "You can't fix stupid."

Perhaps one of the most bizarre videos to sweep the TikTok world was the so-called "cereal challenge." At the time of this writing, the #cerealchallenge has 5.4 million views. In order to participate, you need two people. While one lies flat on their back (preferably on a kitchen counter for ultimate video editing authenticity), the other pours a steady stream of milk into their mouth. When full, they then dump in as much cereal as possible. Some users even go as far as to grab a spoon and try to eat out of their friend's mouth, who all the while is laughing, gagging, and making a mess by spouting milk in the air.

Besides being gross, this trend is dangerous. Teens have choked. And yet, for a slice of TikTok fame, we are willing to engage in risky behaviors like this. The willingness to act like fools to gain the attention of others is so strong; is there anything we won't do?

Apparently not. In 2020, the stupidity limit was pushed to the brink. In fact, it became so big that it made national news. A group of teens got together and decided that it would be a hilarious idea to drop a penny in between an electrical outlet and their phone while it was charging halfway off a wall. Naturally, sparks flew. In addition to blowing up their phones, the "penny challenge" blew up on TikTok.

Thousands of users were suddenly eager to risk bodily harm in the pursuit of fame. The situation became so dangerous that the Massachusetts Department of Fire Services started begging for people to stop—which they did, eventually, as soon as the trend died off in favor of another viral video.

Next, let's dive into viral pranks. Without a doubt, YouTube is king. More than anywhere else on the Internet, YouTube is THE PLACE to find videos of dangerous and stupid stunts. Whether it's swimming with sharks, lighting objects on fire, or wearing a mask and chasing innocent people, videos abound. In the past, pranks were harmless jokes we played on unsuspecting people to get an innocent chuckle. They might involve a momentary scare or bout of confusion. But nobody got hurt.

Thanks to the rise in monetization opportunities on YouTube, pranks can now be lucrative ways to quickly gain followers and build an audience around causing misery to others. We love seeing people get hurt, just as much as we love seeing people behave like train wrecks on the Internet (i.e., Nikocado Avocado, who regularly has mental breakdowns and cries in his videos).

One example of an account pranking for fame is ComedyWolf with 1.04 million subscribers. In their bio, they state, "Hi! I'm ComedyWolf, and on this channel, I'm making funny videos, Gold Digger Pranks, Best Pranks On Internet, Picking Uber Riders, Shampoo Pranks & More!" The theme of these videos is all in good fun. Of course, at the end of the pranks, he reveals that he is filming and, most of the time, everyone involved shares a laugh.

The Eradication of Humanity
By Social Media

But before people realize it's a joke, tensions are high. Obviously, people get angry at being touched without their consent. One man yelled, "What the hell, man?" Others physically go after ComedyWolf and try to assault him in return. The most popular videos feature men chasing each other down the street, shouting and flailing their arms. Funny? We guess so. Dangerous? Absolutely. Human beings are unpredictable. You never know who you are approaching or what they might do.

Besides, since when did it become acceptable to go after strangers and touch their clothes, hats, arms, and cars? For the sake of millions of likes and comments, it seems YouTubers who make money off their viral pranks know no limits. If it makes them popular, then there's nothing they won't do, even if it means getting them thrown in prison or banned from countries.

Logan Paul has been banned from Japan after filming a dead body during his vlog on Aokigahara, a sacred forest in Japan where troubled souls go to die.

Like most social media platforms, TikTok brings a sense of community and togetherness among strangers with similar and common interests. It gives those who often feel left out a sense of belonging and those who feel isolated from the world a sense of comfort and friendship amongst the chaos and shame that public socializing has become.

Getting to know others and making friends in the real world aren't what they used to be. People used to welcome others when they tried to share or open themselves to strangers. Nowadays, if we approach those we don't know, trying to make friends, we are publicly humiliated and shamed. When social media users feel a sense of connection and relatability to those they follow, they're more inclined to stay on the apps so they can feel like they belong in the worlds of those they normally wouldn't.

Furthermore, its diversified content, which is easy to consume, only temporarily quenches the thirst. It leaves users face-to-face with the eternal dilemma of when to stop scrolling, repeatedly saying to themselves, "just one more." And that's how hours later, they're still on TikTok, neglecting everything else they need to do.

Their finger almost moves on its own, going back and forth between the panoply of choices available to them on the app. They keep wondering what kind of video they'd see next if they keep going, and the curiosity is never-ending. This phenomenon must have been recurrent because the creators themselves post videos telling their viewers to take a break. When that happens, you know you have a problem.

Most content that do well on these social platforms consist of simple acts of distraction, those that provide out-of-body experiences that are both catchy and memorable. Most people on social media want apps to provide straight-up fun without worrying or spending time thinking about complicated things (i.e., dance videos usually do better than educational ones).

We all just want that background noise, the quick entertainment we can scroll through, watch for a second, then move onto the next. This is the magic of TikTok, brainwashing magic that fuels the motivation of people to keep them coming back for more, whether that involves hate or love towards certain videos. These subconscious and dark desires of people are what contribute to TikTok fame.

And it's not just us profiting from this endless background noise. Reports of Chinese spyware using the app to gather user's personal information have been on the rise. Since its inception, TikTok has been at the heart of privacy law debates. Last year, a much-anticipated lawsuit was filed in California over the alleged unscrupulous use of surveillance software. Personal data was being collected and stored without consent.

The Eradication of Humanity
By Social Media

We, as users, post our fun little dances and lip-synced songs while being oblivious to the darker aspects.

The situation got so bad that former U.S. President Donald Trump threatened to ban TikTok from being downloaded anywhere in the country. National security professionals all the way up to the FBI were ringing alarm bells about the dangers posed by this app. With tensions already at a boiling point between the U.S. and China in terms of international relations, TikTok found itself at the very heart of a raging debate over information dissemination and data collection.

Almost all apps as big as this one monetize our data. Think about it. If an app is free to download, how are they making money? The answer is terrifying—data mining, selling, and storage through Chinese enterprises. And we're not just talking about information like a person's favorite color. Raw data about every aspect of our lives are being sorted, categorized, and hoarded away for the future by a world superpower with questionable privacy ethics—one who suddenly has access to millions of U.S. citizens' personal information. Social media is no stranger to leaked information, and TikTok is no different.

The first thing to consider is your face. Who sees it? With a reach of billions, the answer is infinite. Unlike Facebook or even Instagram, TikTok propels our identities out into the world at a level never seen before. One of the most troubling claims made in the lawsuit against TikTok was the assertion that the app used close-ups of our faces to gather biometric data, even when the post doesn't go live. This means that all those drafts, all those private videos never shared publicly, still stashed away elements of our personal profiles and exposed them to the world. Why? We may never get the complete answer. But TikTok did settle the case of running unapproved facial recognition technology for a pretty 92 million. For those worried about security, it's a small price to pay.

The Eradication of Humanity
By Social Media

To be fair, Facebook has been accused of similar privacy crimes. Unless you were living under a rock, you probably heard about their data trafficking accusations. In 2018, it came to light that up to 87 million Facebook accounts had been the subjects of invasive data practices at the hands of Cambridge Analytica. Through the use of surveys and profiling, Cambridge Analytica was blamed for using personal information for political advertising, all while missing one important thing – explicit user consent.

If this sounds familiar, good. Almost all social media companies have come under fire for similar controversies, to varying degrees. We could spend this entire book talking about the legality and morality of such decisions, but the argument stands. Practically since its inception, Facebook has repeatedly failed to protect the privacy of users. They tried, of course. Programmers for the technology giant did their best to defend against the bugs, hackers, and bots which naturally sought out easy targets.

Password protection has definitely gotten better over time and with the advancement of public education. More people than ever now know how to secure their accounts and create strong passwords linked to backup devices. But data breaches still happen, including small ones, such as your annoying younger cousin hacking into your account, and large ones, such as the hacking of the U.S. election.

Who's to blame?

At the end of the day, we do it to ourselves.

We are so obsessed with becoming famous on social media that we hardly ever stop to think about the long-term consequences of trusting these companies with our personal information. If a stranger approached us on the street and asked for our name, date of birth, where we went to school, and photos of our family and friends, we would think they were crazy and run in the opposite direction! But when an app does it, we fail to spot the danger and freely hand over even our bank accounts and social security numbers.

Today, TikTok claims that Singapore is the site of backup servers, while it stores most user data strictly on U.S. servers. TikTok has repeatedly denied any involvement of the Chinese government with regards to spyware. Still, private information—such as country location, Internet address, type of device, age, and phone number—is automatically gathered the second we sign up for an account. Yet, TikTok continues to see over 50 million active users from the United States alone.

Chapter Four

The Addiction Cannot Be Ignored

Let's face it. We are all addicted to social media and the Internet. The creation of the smartphone has only made this addiction worse. We so quickly fall into the temptation of the world of possibilities that lie online that simple "quick checks" on our profiles turn into endless hours of wasted life on meaningless content that contributes nothing but entertainment to our lives. We end up scrolling through more videos than we originally intended, reading comments, and sharing them with others by reposting.

This endless and mindless scrolling defeats the original purpose of social media: connecting. Now, it has turned into who can gain the most fame and become the most popular, using bots and paying others to keep up with their active online presence to avoid losing followers. This traps people into becoming disconnected with their lives just for a few bucks. Sometimes our online personas are nothing like who we are in reality. We just feel compelled to keep up with certain appearances to keep our followers entertained, portraying ourselves as mentally deranged or as train wrecks to maintain our popularity.

None is more controversial than Britney Spears. In fact, Hollywood Reporter included her in their "Top 10 Favorite Train Wrecks of All Time: Then and Now" article. Spears joined the TikTok community just two years ago. Since, she has racked up over 4 million followers, with an average view count of 10 million per video. We love her. Those of us who are millennials remember Britney from the good old days of "Oops!...I Did It Again" and "Baby One More Time."

She personifies the quintessential angel fallen from grace. Though her personal problems began long before TikTok, it has proven to be the platform of choice in what GenZ calls her "cry for help." In extremely intimate videos, wearing booty shorts, a bikini, or dark ringed eyeshadow, Britney regularly posts clips of herself showing off yoga or dance moves. She simultaneously looks confused and exhausted while boasting an unnaturally fake smile.

To an outsider, the desperation in her eyes is chilling. We don't care. We hit like, we send hearts, we interact and comment on each video by the millions, all in some deranged attempt to gorge the beast. She is sad. She needs our attention, we tell ourselves. She craves our support for the sake of her mental health. The irony being, of course, that in doing so, we keep this already popular celebrity in the limelight by perpetuating an endless cycle of social media addiction.

At the end of the day, did we truly help anyone, or are we only driving the pop star into a deeper state of depression?

Chapter Five

We're Disconnected From Reality

As an extension of Internet addiction, social media addiction has long been a compulsive disorder where people use social media to extreme excess. Without going into the details of the actual figures or how it has already impacted the lives of millions, what can be said is that social media addiction is real and fatal; and TikTok may be on its way to becoming the most virulent and widespread social network of all time.

However, this phenomenon is not unknown to people. More than 12% of active social media users experience, to some extent, the symptoms of addiction. Although most are aware of their dependency on the apps, they find themselves drawn into them for entertainment and recognition anyway, a reality that eventually hits them so hard that they struggle to remove themselves.

But they're not to blame. Most of us live mundane lives that leave us unmotivated to break out of, work 9 to 5 jobs, and come home to alcohol and television. Social apps allow us to feel like we're a part of something beyond ourselves while remaining in our comfort zones as introverts. An online presence allows us to be someone else, someone aside from our true selves that we're not ashamed of.

We use social media to find love and acceptance in a world that has become highly antisocial. When we're isolated and forgotten in reality, we turn to the Internet for comfort, the number of followers seen as friends. It's unfortunate how desperate we can be to gain followers because we want to feel like we matter, though there are still cases where people have let fame get into their heads and become entitled.

Those are the ones who have gone too far in to save.

With the current global pandemic that is COVID-19 and the crash of society in 2020, many social network users turned to social platforms as their only escape route from the endless boredom that was quarantine. They tried to find ways to stay connected with the world without physically having to leave their homes, not like many of them left their homes to begin with. But since quarantine began, many have attempted to find hobbies that allowed them to stay indoors since outdoor activities, such as dining out and traveling, were off the plate.

The Eradication of Humanity
By Social Media

Sadly, many became social sheep, starting OnlyFans accounts and twerking on camera instead of doing something more productive.

Is this really what the world can turn into when we're forced to disconnect from others?

Is this what the world will become decades from now?

Are we destined only to live socially and virtually?

Or can we learn to communicate with others in public once again without becoming the next biggest cringe?

I don't want to harsh on TikTok too much, as it did bring some light and positivity to people when they were struggling. TikTok allowed people to channel their creativity and stay sane while the world around them came crashing down. It was something people really needed in order to remain confident in what the future could bring when there were uncertainties left and right. With many laid off from their jobs or forced to continue their education at home, more and more people turned to TikTok as a way to portray their presence during a time when they were forced to shut themselves off from others.

However, there was no way of predicting how far many others would take the app, including filming TikTok videos at work, leading to them getting fired for publicly broadcasting confidential information. Or filming TikTok videos in public and ignoring all social distancing rules for the sake of being seen as "pretty" and "cultured."

Case after case has proven that we will ignore others in search for fame. Given the opportunity, we will step on the backs of innocent people to lift ourselves upwards, an inch closer to the light that is the pursuit of fame and glory. We see it all the time. Friends who get along perfectly well in real life will suddenly turn on one another online to cause drama, stir the proverbial pot, and get attention from their classmates. Likewise, we have all seen videos taken of people at their absolute worst, just to make fun of them and collectively laugh at their misfortune.

We tell ourselves this is okay because it gets us closer to the popularity we so desire.

Hurt is temporary.

But in our minds, fame is forever.

Tim Redman found out the hard way why filming TikToks at work is a bad idea. After working at a hotel for just over a year, he was fired. His termination came as a result of him posting videos making fun of guests checking into Hilton hotels. In a flippant manner, he bragged about upgrading rooms for hotel guests who were cheating on their spouses. He also boasted about watching elderly couples skinny-dipping in the pool.

When called out by a coworker for his inappropriate actions, he posted a video of himself "crying" and wrote, "Please guys...help me out. Please take me back, Hilton. I didn't mean to cause any harm." In his power play for fame, Redman ignored the pain he was causing others. His company exposed him as an unreliable employee. In just minutes, he lost a job he loved. We should all take note.

But as recent studies and demographics have shown, even before the unprecedented situation of the deadly virus, the average time spent by TikTok users on the app was 52 minutes, so quarantine life is not solely to blame. Also, many users acknowledge that they are way over this threshold.

They admit that they can keep scrolling for several hours in a row without feeling the need to stop because they are having fun, especially during the holidays when they're not obligated to focus on anything else except for their family. But we all know we're spending time with our real families less and less while spending more and more time with our online families. That's the power of the Internet.

The addiction is so bad that if we continue to browse through the app without taking a break, videos posted by TikTok itself would pop up saying things like, "You're still here? Take a break, read a book, do some exercise. Don't worry. I will be here when you get back!" Do they mean it, or is it just a tactic to avoid blame and survive the backlash they would get for the recurring effects that their app is having on its users? They could then clear themselves and wipe the responsibility off their hands, saying that they have warned people as much as possible. Emphasis on "as much as possible."

Soon after its launch, TikTok added a feature that enabled its users to limit their time on the app. They had four different choices, ranging from 40 to 120 minutes, which can only be seen as alarming since no other app has ever demonstrated the need for its users to be called back to reality. They forget to eat and end up engaging in this repetitive cycle every single day. They also manifest other symptoms of addiction, such as an unavoidable urge to log onto the app as they see it as essential and crucial to their lifestyles.

Many of us trying to make a living off of social media alone, the income lifestyle of the new generation, become anxious and self-conscious about our content. Therefore, we constantly feel the need to check up on our own profiles or feeds to see if people like our material or not. It's like how we feel when we put up an Instagram post of a cute picture of ourselves that we try to pull off as "took this by accident."

We're self-conscious, and when we put a video or picture up of ourselves that is not well received, we become terrified that people hate it, and we quickly take it down. Half the time we spend on TikTok and other social media is to monitor what others think about our posts. We feel a slight ego boost from those who like our content, and we delete the people who don't.

The Eradication of Humanity
By Social Media

How far will we go to achieve the slightest of fame and attention? Many of us already see our mental health and intelligence go down as we lose sleep, and we become so invested in our social lives that we no longer know the difference between real or fake. But many of us have also turned to backstabbing and shitting on those we love so we can go viral, murdering others to entertain strangers or hurting ourselves just to get others to notice us.

There is no end in sight as to how far we will go. Students will film their teachers in class and secretly post content without their knowledge. They will belittle and bully the adults in their lives, bemoaning the very existence of the adults trying to help them.

Siblings terrorize one another for clout.

Divorced mothers and fathers attack their ex-partners, publicly shaming them and airing the dirty laundry to complete strangers.

Even doctors aren't immune—medical professionals have lost their licenses for sharing confidential information about their patients.

We will stop at nothing.

It's the small price for fame.

The worst part is that most of us aren't even aware of how much time we waste in front of our screens. One hour quickly turns into three, four, or five. If we spend eight hours sleeping (if that even happens anymore), there's not much time left to be productive on anything else, resulting in our work etiquette and education suffering. And all as a result of trying to boost our egos, causing us to lose motivation and have nothing left once the Internet is taken away from us. Other symptoms of social media addiction can manifest in interpersonal problems, such

The Eradication of Humanity
By Social Media

as permanent distancing from people in real life, resulting in low self-esteem when the only "friends" we have left are those on the Internet who can turn on us within minutes.

Chapter Six

Do We Really Care about the Issues We Promote, or is it All for Fame and Attention?

We all want to live in a safe world. That goes without saying. But with incidents of racial injustice on the rise, social media proves to have an important role to play. How we respond to

The Eradication of Humanity
By Social Media

one of the greatest challenges of our generation isn't a question to think about tomorrow – it's already here.

Let's go to the Discover Bar of TikTok at the time of this writing. Did you notice how "Stop Anti-Asian Racism" is the trending banner? This isn't accidental. Anti-Asian hate crimes rose by 30% in 2020. Every day, we see and hear racial discussions on the news and radio, but social media is a different creature. In this space, people can be unfiltered with their innermost thoughts. The net is cast so wide that somebody is bound to agree with you no matter what you say.

And thanks to the algorithm, TikTok will clump us all together based on our similarities. Before long, we only see what we want to see; our biases are confirmed. By removing those who disagree with us, we are convinced that we were right all along. If someone with contrasting views slips through the cracks, we just block them or shadowban them. Problem solved. This is a very attractive feature for racists seeking an audience. It's no longer about freedom of speech. It's now about promoting speech we know others will want to hear, even if we don't believe the words we promote.

It's now all about the "best things" we can say to get others to follow us.

Just look at the case of George Floyd—#georgefloyd has 4.8 billion views. Millions upon millions of videos exist of people discussing the details of his death. Everyone, from the average citizen to lawyers, judges, and police officers, is talking about what happened. And they're using TikTok to get their voices out.

We all do the same thing.

We scream and shout; we wave flags and don colorful buttons representing issues we often know little about.

The Eradication of Humanity
By Social Media

We call ourselves the "warriors" of social justice, attend rallies, and confront our enemies.

After all, this is *our* platform.

We are the new generation, and we are going to be the change.

TikTok amplifies our voices to be far louder than ever imagined.

But let's be real. How often do we see people at these protests spending the entire time staring down at their phones? Or filming the event as it unfolds in some sort of exposé that they themselves are the stars of? Quite often, people infiltrate BLM or anti-Asian hate protests not to help, but to catapult themselves onto center stage, a vain attempt to garner attention away from the issue and onto themselves. In doing so, we detract from the real problems and, instead, play a never-ending game of, "Who is more woke?"

Let's not forget the controversy of Kris Schatzel, an influencer who came under fire for using a Black Lives Matter protest as her own personal photoshoot, walking in the opposite direction of other protestors and posing for cameras.

If we really cared, we would remove ourselves from the equation. Activism isn't meant to be selfish. It isn't meant to be a photoshoot. Yet, it very often descends into just that, with people taking advantage of serious situations for their own personal gain.

So, what did TikTok do in the face of BLM and growing anti-Asian opinions? The company took a public stance against racism, not a very convincing one, but strong compared to Facebook and Twitter, who, some say, don't do nearly enough to combat hateful language on their platforms. Instead, TikTok made a call to be anti-racist and invited us to report others for racist abuse. We could post video clips of ourselves boasting about how we are allies; we could protest together at BLM rallies and play it back over catchy music. We could create hashtags such as: #blacklivesmatter and #IamNOTAVIRUS. We were able to show solidarity and use our #ownvoices to show that we "did the work."

Emphasis on "we." As with all social media, the onus is on the user to engage thoughtfully and appropriately. TikTok may not encourage racist behavior, but it certainly doesn't seek to weed it out either. There is a fine line between censorship and freedom of speech. For TikTok, the company's answer was to institute a banner and a "report" button.

Is this enough to stop the hate?

Chapter Seven

Social Media is Fake, and So Are We

We use TikTok to brag and show an idealistic portrait of life. TikTok is like a double-edged sword. Depending on its user (the person wielding the weapon), it becomes a weapon that can prove fatal. And not necessarily for others, but more so for the wielder. It may provide short-lived relief, but it's not a cure for what's eating the person up from the inside. We constantly use social media as a distraction from the real troubles that pain us in life.

Low self-esteem is not something a person can easily heal or grow out of. It is like a second skin, one that some people can't get accustomed to. It's like looking in the mirror and not being able to recognize your reflection. It involves everything from a negative self-image, self-hatred, and feelings of worthlessness to oversensitivity and perfectionism. It is something that wears us out, reinforcing our already existent tendencies to criticize and belittle our every choice, word, and action. It is nothing short of exhausting, almost impossible to be treated on its own.

And social media doesn't make it any easier to deal with. When we put ourselves on the Internet, our raw selves, we're exposing our vulnerabilities to the world. That's why we always try to get the best angles of ourselves, to show others only what we want to show them because those parts will bring us the points we need to boost our egos. We purposefully give people the content that we know will generate the most attention, so any likes we receive automatically will boost our self-esteem.

Unfortunately, this can often backfire; believe it or not, there are people out there who don't think we're top shit. There's no way of preventing people from disliking us regardless of how hard we try, and the more this happens, the more we try to change their opinions, and the lower our confidence drops. Eventually, we no longer recognize ourselves because we have spent all our time pleasing those we don't even know.

No one is real on Instagram, but the hate certainly is. Of all social media choices, Instagram has some of the worst messages. Judgmental comments are out of control. Just search #ugly to see the self-deprecating posts people are driven to make. Instagram has become the "pièce de résistance" for shallow, vain, beauty-driven content. As users, we know this, and we feed off it.

The Eradication of Humanity
By Social Media

Because the app thrives on photographs, we are always searching for the next outfit, makeup, backdrop, or pose that will get us noticed. Our images compete with thousands uploaded by the minute; there's simply no way to avoid comparing ourselves to our rivals. No matter what, something we post is going to annoy somebody else. In turn, this leads to poor body image.

You could be the most beautiful and kindhearted person in the whole universe. Guess what? On Instagram, it counts for nothing. The haters will find you, and given the chance, they'll tear your self-confidence to shreds.

Just look at the trolls. On www.howtogeek.com, an Internet troll is defined as "someone who makes intentionally inflammatory, rude, or upsetting statements online to elicit strong emotional responses in people or to steer the conversation off-topic." Trolls can be anyone. A random person, or someone we know more intimately hiding behind their phone screen.

At 222 million followers, Selena Gomez knows this better than anyone. In 2019, the celebrity uninstalled Instagram from her phone. Her reason? Negativity from Internet trolls clashing with her fans in the comments section. She began to feel depressed on the platform. During an interview on LIVE with Kelly & Ryan, Gomez said, "I think it's just become really unhealthy for young people, including myself, to spend all their time fixating on all these comments."

If a talented singer and celebrity can be driven to delete social media because of relentless bullying, imagine the harm it can cause to an impressionable teen. The influencer's advice? Don't feed the trolls. But when our identities are so caught up in perpetuating the fairytale of social media, it's hard, and we find ourselves in the face of death after it's too late.

The Eradication of Humanity
By Social Media

We all want to be someone other than ourselves because we never took the time to discover who we are. Social media no longer represents a platform where we can freely express ourselves. It has become an empty hole where we are censored for offending others, and those we strive to become aren't even real.

From an early age, we're told we can be anything we want to be. We dream about future careers. We imagine life as an astronaut, writer, scientist, or veterinarian. As children, we are so eager to grow up! The world is our oyster, and there is nothing we can't accomplish.

But then the teenage years hit. Suddenly, everyone is judging everybody else. There are strange, new rules, and a social hierarchy is established. All the little pieces that make us special, that make us unique, quickly become much less significant.

What if others don't approve?

What if we don't fit in with the crowd?

The repercussions are real. So, to avoid running the risk of being labeled an "outcast," we morph into a version of ourselves that we think others want to see. It isn't real. But that doesn't matter.

We think the easiest way to deal with our imperfections and flaws is to hide them, ignore them, and only focus on the things we choose to. We actively choose to neglect the damaged parts of our lives and enhance the parts we believe are likeable, to the point where even we begin to think we're perfect and that those constructed features are real.

With this type of mentality and content, when we choose to flex, we're cheating ourselves and our viewers into having them think the impossible is achievable. Hiding behind filters and Photoshop to make ourselves look better only serves as an injustice when our fans see us in public, and we look nothing like how we do online.

Like Tana Mongeau and her infamous flat stomach on social media that looks completely different from her actual body, or video streamers who replace their faces with those of conventional beauty and completely flop when they get exposed, we become unrecognizable to ourselves and those who know us, using so many filters and makeup that our real faces start to look foreign.

Social media has become a deceptive lie, and TikTok is no different. Contrary to what other people may think about those "perfect" videos, there is nothing for them to be jealous about or envious of. Not everyone resorts to this kind of method, of course, in order to achieve the satisfaction and comfort this ephemeral fame may bring them. Some people have made it to their perfect place through blood, tears, and extraordinary effort.

But they are swamped in the ocean of other illusory "perfect" stories others are telling, their achievements undervalued. How tragic is it that people might even change themselves to resemble one of those who pretend, one of those who are struggling even more so than themselves? Whatever happened to perfection through hard work, not just advanced app and filter skills?

Yet, everyone has imperfections, and deep down, we all know that. Instead of simply admitting them, nowadays, people try to hide behind fake decor, lies, secrets, thick makeup, surgeries, and editing, just to name a few. Instead of accepting and proclaiming body positivity, instead of spreading acceptance and love for what they truly are inside, they decide to hide.

Why not give beauty the treatment it deserves, as it eventually fades away with age and wrinkles? People would rather blame themselves for not being perfect like the augmented people they see online. They are judgmental with their own bodies but would praise another's body for its flaws. They are perfectionists who don't set realistic expectations for themselves and sweat the small stuff, not understanding that failing doesn't make them a failure.

Recently, many teenagers and young adults have posted on the app about relativity and positivity, saying out loud for everyone to hear that everybody is beautiful and deserves to be cherished. Now, although this sounds like a gem and body positivity at first, it's just another bullshit way for people to gain attention. Saying "everyone is beautiful" can be just as damaging as it is inspirational.

The body positivity movement has gotten so out of hand that healthy is now seen as a sin, and these activists promote the obesity lifestyle as one to envy. This not only inspires people to stay unhealthy in their bodies, but it also creates an unreasonable level of self-confidence that encourages us to go against the standard conventional means of beauty, even if it means eating (or starving) ourselves to death.

Eating disorders aren't immune to social media. Though this medical disorder flourishes in secrecy, issues such as Anorexia and Bulimia have found a comfortable home on Instagram. A quick search for #edrecovery will show a whopping 4 million posts. This is irrefutable proof that Instagram is not – we repeat, *is not* – able to control posts about the mental or physical well-being of its users.

Sure, if you search #anorexia, a warning pops up. "Resources That Might Help" appears. One click later, and there is a "content advisory" that says the app wants to protect "our community from content that may encourage harmful behavior." But pros know how to get around this. Just misspell anorexia. Use a French hyphen above the I. As if by magic, skinny legs and protruding ribs abound.

The Eradication of Humanity
By Social Media

We yammer for body positivity but ignore the reality. The reality is that we are obsessed with followers and likes and will do anything for attention. #fitspo has 73 million posts, more of a cult and another body obsession than a healthy lifestyle. Nothing is off-limits. Before and after photos, meals, workout videos, weight gain/loss, and barely-there clothes are shared for all to see.

Like all social media, TikTok still promotes an unreasonable standard of beauty and appearance, saying that to become big and noticed, women still need to behave in provocative manners while men still need to assert their dominance. Even when we try to promote something other than the standard, many of us still secretly hold onto that mantra that we must be and look like certain types of people. Body positivity seems to ring true only for people when there's a following behind it.

Behind the scenes, most of us are still self-conscious about our bodies.

In the end, TikTok offers superficial content, just like Instagram does. Everything revolves around beauty to entice others to adhere to similar trends. Clothing, hairstyle, makeup, or attitude, everything is calculated for a perfect result—a beautiful, skilled, respectful, generous, organized, and patient identity, close to perfection.

Many different applications were later added in response to this growing need for flawlessness and supremacy, despite already being implemented on other social media apps.

For instance, we could talk about easy editing of photographs and videos, adding fake backgrounds and lighting, adding quick and colorful filters over our images, retouching our faces and body proportions, dashboard previews and harmonization, marketing assistants for social media, captions easy to apply on video, programming posts assistants, etc. The list goes on as new functionalities arise and requirements increase. People are even now making a living from this, putting their Photoshopping skills to use to generate income from those superficial enough to pay them to enhance breasts, shrink waists, and plop them in Disneyland.

There will always be people who strive to become influencers despite what it takes, including filming houses and cars of other people and playing them off as their own, or filming only certain angles to lie about how much they actually have. As long as people are willing to pay for this type of content, people will sell them, like allowing hopefuls to rent out the set of a private plane for clout.

Fame and wealth are no longer about who brings the most talent to the table; it has turned into who can portray the best version of themselves rather than living up to their true abilities. We even go as far as trashing our friends and family online if it means the controversy has the potential of going viral.

However, this hungry desire for attention is not necessarily out of malice or bad intentions. We just so happen to live in a society where this is expected of us, and we're surrounded by people who make it difficult for us to socialize and live otherwise. We're all struggling, and we see social media as a potential way out of our misery. Whereas some may say that this variety of platforms emphasizes open-mindedness, others argue that it exacerbates the obsession and thirst.

Despite everyone knowing that the fame we see on social media is born from lies and fabrication, we still implement the fake strategies and tips people share just to attract attention or to feel powerful for changing the life of another human being. As is the case for many tutors or mentors on TikTok, we still chase after this impossible dream. We try to convince people that we are successful and better than everyone else because of the things we pretend to have.

But how true is that?

The Eradication of Humanity
By Social Media

We live in a world of lies, brainwashed into thinking we can become rich and famous the easy way instead of working hard like people used to do.

What happened to honesty and integrity?

Nowadays, it seems like almost anyone can become famous, with beauty and fetishes topping the charts on who gets noticed the most.

What happens when social media perishes?

What's next?

Porn?

People act as if they were building a machine out of spare parts, like putting together another persona whose characteristics we freely pick and choose. And the whiter the canvas, the riskier it is for them to try to reinvent themselves by copying the unruly and unhealthy things others do. Although the terms of use of the application set the minimum age for subscription at 13, it is widely known to all users that many children still view the content.

Younger and younger children interact with TikTok, whether it's because they lie about their age or their parents expose them for fame. We go on TikTok and see children prancing around in provocative outfits. Children are gaining access to phones and social media younger and younger these days, to the point where a lot are already in the spotlight before they even get a chance to grow up.

TikTok, in response to the growing worry, tried harnessing the power of AI to filter the videos children would have access to, improving its restricted viewing mode function. But the problem lies elsewhere, as they can never have 100% control over it.

The Eradication of Humanity
By Social Media

Should these children really be scrolling through the pile of visual anguish and luxury that certain people indulge in?

Should these young children rely on the amusement of social media instead of playing with toys and going out with friends?

Are these children able to differentiate what they should and shouldn't look to as examples, and can they separate irony and sarcasm from real advice?

Most children don't know how to protect themselves from the influence of strangers.

But are parents ready to take the blame and bear the consequences?

No. The answer to all those questions is no.

Social media has corrupted the innocence of children, such as the controversies with Danielle Cohn and Zoe Laverne, among others, from excessive skin exposure to kissing minors. Childhood innocence is under attack and has been for quite some time. Suddenly, little girls and boys are imitating grown women and men.

Think about how common it is now to hear children use swear words on the Internet. Toddlers as young as three are recorded by their parents, who then post videos on TikTok of their child saying "fuck" or "shit" for the first time, hoping to grab some attention and likes. We laugh.

How cute! How adorable! These silly children don't know what they're saying. It's funny!

A few hours later, the video has collected thousands of views. What once occurred in the privacy of one's own home, and would be used as a parent-child teachable moment, is now cheapened. How desperate must we be to use our children as bait for clout?

If you want to know, just take a look at the hashtag #kidsswearing on TikTok. Among the first videos that pop up is one of a mother doing her makeup in front of the mirror. While dotting her nose with powder, she struggles to hold both the camera and her squirming child. As her little girl mumbles along to the ABCs, she suddenly screams a loud, "fuck!"

Rather than using this opportunity to be surprised, the mother instead bursts out laughing and writes #fbomb before posting the clip on her account. What could have been a private moment of humor between a parent and child is now made public for the world to criticize and judge. It isn't the child's fault. She is just trying to learn.

Are we making a mountain out of a molehill? Maybe. But consider that, in the bio line of this user's account, she has a link for, "How to Become an Influencer." Using your infant daughter to garner attention is, it appears, a tried-and-true strategy for success.

That is just one example. But all children, from toddlers right up to late teens, feel the pressure to trade their precious innocence for hearts and likes.

They are not able, aware, or ready to go through that and make those choices. Since values and judgement are born from experience and mistakes, they are too ill-equipped to be handling those responsibilities, as childish and harmless as they may seem. Take Lil Tay, for example, a once-child star known for flexing her "wealth" is now in the middle of a domestic abuse controversy, growing up too fast to stay out of the Internet's eyes.

Children often copy parents and adults because, to them, they are figures of authority—people they must obey and who, therefore, dictate good conduct. They will automatically reproduce something they see on a video if they like it, without knowing how wrong it is. For them, it is inconceivable that some people show things they shouldn't do on video. They are innocent and trusting. That is something that should be preserved and handled with care.

The content they have access to needs to be monitored to avoid ruining their innocence and polluting their minds with filth. Children are sponges that absorb feelings, ideas, speech patterns, and even behaviors from those they meet, watch, or hold close. They don't know yet who they really are; they are trying to build themselves. Being a copycat only confuses them further, delaying their emotional growth until it might be too late to remedy.

Children are no longer protected from NSFW content on the Internet, especially when parents use them as lures for attention or as their own personal cameramen.

Livestreaming is especially risky. Parents can't monitor their child's online behavior all the time, and with creator's streaming live videos 24/7, keeping an eye on what their son or daughter is watching becomes impossible.

Consider Twitch. At any time of day or night, we can log on. Just over 80% of the users identify as male, making this social media platform more likely to attract young boys. In addition, most Twitch users are between 18-34 years old. This isn't our grandma's app. It's new, fresh, juvenile, and has all the trappings of being highly addictive. Much of the content are inappropriate for vulnerable and impressionable kids, admiring people like Eugenia Cooney and aspiring to starve themselves to be as thin as the Anorexic star in denial.

Let's look at the "Just Chat" feature. While Twitch is best known for video games, these kinds of streams are different because they let people, well...just chat. About anything.

Creators sometimes use their downtime between games to have conversations with their fans. Other times, people will film themselves watching a TV show or cooking a meal.

Seemingly innocent enough, these chat sessions are ripe for abuse. Since chat participants are anonymous with only screen names to identify them, it's way too easy for trolls, haters, or even pedophiles to send inappropriate messages. People can ask, "What's your name?" or "Where do you go to school?", and there's no safeguard to stop a child from answering with the truth. Likewise, racial slurs and homophobic comments are rampant.

Twitch does try to ban people for inappropriate language. But with constant streaming, it's hard to catch them all. Plus, it's on us to report any violations. More often than not, we shrug it off as a necessary evil for livestreaming.

But surely the dangers of Twitch end there?

Afraid not.

To make a Twitch account and live stream, you can be as young as thirteen. Not even old enough to legally drive! That means kids still in middle school can be watched in their homes, in real-time, by absolute strangers. It's not that much of a stretch to say this is comparable to a lurker creeping outside a child's bedroom window and spying on him or her. Because that's exactly what's happening – only online. We might as well hang a sign saying, "pedophiles welcome."

And that's just the dangers the viewers present. What does the research say about the streamers themselves? To start, many users are gamers who spend 15-20 hours streaming. Spending this much time in front of a screen isn't good for our health. We know lack of physical activity leads to long-term and poor health outcomes, like obesity. Pair that with an obsession, and we have an addiction in the making. Also, don't forget: even though we might be talking to dozens of people, social isolation is still a real problem.

Lots of streamers report feeling lonely, despite sitting online with fans for hours and hours. Why? Because fans aren't friends that we can talk to and confide in. They are strangers we are performing for. This isn't normal; it's not how human beings were made to interact. We don't like it, and yet, we can't stop.

Additionally, it's not just about whether or not the child is a streamer or is a viewer interacting with the streamer. People in the chats talk to each other, so they can be preyed upon by other viewers. A lot depends on how good the streamers or mods are about catching them and banning them, or giving them a time out.

It's no exaggeration to say this is damaging to young minds. Recently, TikTok has come under fire because of graphic content. Despite the app's best efforts to catch gruesome images before they travel too far, there have been cases where clips of accidental death or suicide made it to the public For You Page. Unbeknownst to us, as we mindlessly scroll for hours, a video would open showing us NSFW content we might not want to see.

We absorb the images and sounds before we can stop them or scroll away. Some adults have said they suffered from PTSD, such as in the case of the TikToker who captured footage of seven college students dying when a balcony collapsed. The video was removed, but not before it was shared thousands of times.

We wonder: how many children saw that video?

Chapter Eight

It Doesn't Matter If We're Dead...As Long As We're Famous

But all users, conflicted with self-esteem and addiction, are just as fragile as these young children. Their age matters little because they are all damaged. Some of them never even notice.

The Eradication of Humanity
By Social Media

They hide their insecurities behind a persona they project onto the world, trying to make it true. In the end, the fine line between virtual life and reality becomes more and more blurry. And somehow, that is what they want—for the fake and fabricated reality to fuse with the real one. And this fake life begins to grow stronger. They always hope to get closer and closer to their dreamy expectations until they ultimately realize it was all futile.

Social media is fake, just another app. We need to remember that this is a digital imprint based in a digital world. While the emotions conjured up during our participation on social media are certainly real, their legitimacy is built upon an extraordinarily shaky ground. If the Internet disappeared tomorrow, who knows what the long-term effects would be on our sense of self?

To an addicted adolescent brimming with the desire to reach an unrealistic level of fame, the danger is ever so present. For the sole purpose of getting a large number of views to become an influencer with a huge community of followers, these inexperienced teenagers, with no real sense of self, could not, and would not, refrain from posting sensitive content on the Internet.

They want to fit into the mold, resemble others they do not know in real life, and go to any lengths with that in mind. After all, all they want is to feel good about themselves.

We have become so desperate to fit in, so willing to sell our souls to the devil, that we give away our personal information and identity for that chance at belonging. We become so desperate that we don't even notice that we're potentially putting our lives at risk. Take the example of Alexis Sharkey, an Instagram influencer found dead on the side of a road.

Alexis Sharkey was only twenty-six years old when she was murdered. As a beloved influencer, she would post pictures and videos of her fashion and leisure lifestyle around the Houston area. Her death was immediately deemed suspicious, which raises the question: how safe are we when we share our regular hangout locations with strangers over social media?

If you want to know how dangerous TikTok stalkers can be, just go to Reddit. There are threads upon threads of people sharing their stories. Ex-boyfriends, random folks in the grocery store, and even our own "friends" have been caught stalking our profiles. We make it so easy for them, posting about our jobs, where we live, and our favorite restaurants.

We film beside our cars, sometimes not even bothering to crop out the license plate number, and we do tours of our houses, expertly laying out a map of door and window entrances for any burglar to see. We turn ourselves into the easiest of targets without even thinking about it.

And TikTok can provide this illusion for them. It includes, as one of its main attractions, challenges and memes that many reproduce since they tend to go viral very quickly. Some involve dancing, fitness, and painting, while others involve tricking family and friends to see their reactions. People are always looking for new ways to stand out, creating new challenges and, sadly, sometimes out of dangerous, unsafe, or uncomfortable practices that later lead to serious incidents. Some of them are sexually suggestive, while others are outright dangerous, resulting in death for the most tragic cases. But is that enough to scare this bold generation away? It seems not.

Mary-Belle Kirschner, or Belle Delphine, is an Internet celebrity. Using primarily Snapchat and YouTube, she built an empire. Delphine figured out that she could monetize her body by modeling, doing erotic baby doll cosplays, and selling, not only images of herself, but also her bath water to some of her 1.95 million subscribers. At one point, she was even banned from YouTube for violating guidelines on sexual content. It begs the question: is social media really the place to sell pornographic work? Or should that be left to adult websites dedicated to providing such content?

We can cite a few examples of these dangerous practices, such as the "Condom Challenge," which consists of breathing in a condom through your nose at the risk of asphyxiation, or the "Neck Your Drink," which includes consuming extremely strong alcohol (naturally, this does not go without its own consequences). Unfortunately, the latter resulted in the death of 5 young teenagers, who tragically indulged in these practices despite the dangers. Who could've predicted that a social media app could lead to such tragedy?

There are many, many more. You don't need to be a pharmacist to know that taking massive doses of any drug can kill you. Chloe Phillips, a fifteen-year-old teenager, died after participating in the so-called "Benadryl Challenge" on TikTok. It was rumored on social media that ingesting large amounts of antihistamines could lead to trippy hallucinations. Benadryl became the drug of choice for viral videos, thanks to its easy access as a common allergy medication. Chloe wasn't intentionally trying to kill herself, but she died nevertheless. Her family pleaded with others to be smarter than their daughter, lest they too end up in the emergency room or the morgue.

TikTok wins for short viral challenges. For longer ones, YouTube takes the cake. At the height of its popularity, the "Chubby Bunny" challenge was all the rage. It involved stuffing as many marshmallows into your mouth as possible, then saying "chubby bunny." The marshmallows stick together in a gooey mess, so everyone laughs at the person's attempt at speaking clearly.

The sisters from a TLC hit show, "1,000 Pound Sisters," decided it would be fun to try. Their video received over two million views! Luckily, for these girls, nothing bad happened (except the continued glorification of unhealthy eating habits).

The Eradication of Humanity
By Social Media

But another woman died from trying the same thing. In a similar marshmallow-eating contest, Janet Rudd shoved so many marshmallows in her mouth that she obstructed her airway. Even with an emergency medical team on site, she couldn't be saved. Again, this shows how we will do literally anything for attention, including participating in stupid challenges that we *know* are dangerous.

The "Scalp Popping," for instance, is a challenge that consists of quickly pulling the skin away from the bones. That creates a vacuum as the leftover space is filled with liquid. But many doctors have objected to this particular practice, because pulling too hard by mistake could lead to tearing the tissue or the skin, losing a lot of hair in the process. It is, by no means, healthy and should be left to trained professionals, and there could be a victim in the near future if these experiments continue.

The "Skull Breaker" is another recent challenge that medical practitioners have acknowledged as reckless and dangerous. They were right. The "Skull Breaker Challenge," which involves two people fooling a third into jumping in the air, just to kick their feet out from under them, endangered the lives of several adolescents, who ended up in the hospital after throwing their friends to the ground head first without any way to ease the fall.

We can also cite three other challenges which involve women, making one gender no less stupid than the other. The first one involves pushing their breasts together to show off their cleavage, and the second one, "Invisible Filter," encourages the user to get naked in front of the camera with only a light, transparent, blurry filter to cover their whole body. The third one involves taking all their clothes off, head down, with only their feet.

But the question is, can this generation even be blamed?

The Eradication of Humanity
By Social Media

Do we blame the people or the influences?

Are we just a generation destined to become so vulnerable to following trends that we lose the ability to think for ourselves?

Many users will unintentionally start some silly and thoughtless trend while putting themselves at risk, not expecting people to remake it at home or possibly die because of it. No trend is ever intended to end up like that.

Every generation thinks they are smarter than the one who came before. Human history has taught us that we all share the same innate desire to be loved, and a sense of belonging is crucial. We are primarily social creatures, craving each other's company and acceptance. The difference now is that, with 21st Century technology, how we seek out these connections has changed. Challenges are the latest way to fit in.

However, these challenges generate interest and several million views in just a few days. Influenceable young people cannot escape the dangers of this application by themselves, even when warned. They often do not see the repercussions of their behaviors until it's too late to amend them. Only after they have been hurt, and have possibly hurt others, for the short rush and the fake "happiness" they get from their social profiles, do they understand the foolishness of their acts.

People suffering from social media addiction, and those who take the "fake life" they expose on social media way too seriously, are living a lie—fake happiness that could be easily taken from them without warning. Why do they settle for a fake when they can have a real one? Well, the question should be: could they really?

Teenagers experience considerable stress and anxiety due to the expectations they and their parents have for their future. Homework and exam periods are particularly painful for most of them. They are told to study hard and to get good grades without a valid explanation that really registers with them.

Despite many turning to social media to decrease their stressors from everyday life, social media actually increases anxiety and depression among teens and young adults. The constant trolling and online bullying that pressure us to remove or replace the content we thought was great take a toll on our self-confidence as we constantly try to please those who can't be pleased.

As mentioned previously, rates of depression are on the rise. In an MIT Technology Review, one study found that teens become anxious and depressed after just three hours of social media per day. In addition, teens who spend that much time online are more likely to show signs of aggression and anti-social behavior. The debate is over. We are no longer arguing whether or not excessive social media usage is good or bad for mental health. The evidence is clear. The higher a person's social media usage per day, the poorer their health outcomes.

And in a perverse twist, TikTok has almost embraced this, with hashtags such as #depressiontiktok having 3.3 million views. A secondary hashtag, #depressionsucks, has a whopping 33.3 million. How did we get here? We are so out of touch with what good mental health feels like that we engage with a platform that worsens our mental health struggles. Most frightening of all, children and teenagers don't have the skills or life experience yet to even understand this.

The other thing to think about is, once again, reputation. What we post when we are young does not necessarily represent the adults we become. Looking back, we scoff at the cringe-worthy content our thirteen-year-old selves thought was #cool. Those bathroom mirror selfies with thick black eyeliner? Or poems we wrote about unrequited love in seventh grade? What about those drunken pictures at an underage party? Yikes.

The Eradication of Humanity
By Social Media

As children, we don't have the brain capacity to understand how our future selves might be affected by what we post. We are so obsessed with carving out an identity on social media that we never stop to wonder about the permanency of that identity. As we age and mature, so do our online presence. The things we shared before can't be erased. As adults, we know better, but as children, we don't.

Kids are not prepared ahead of time for the harsh life they will have to lead later on as adults. Schools don't give them the essential tools to do so, but education is not everything in life, especially if they wreck their mental health and happiness in the process. Unfortunately, many parents make this mistake in the hope of paving the way for their child's success. The latter often feel stuck in their lives, with no way to achieve their goals and no prospects. They are living in a closed-off space, in which, for them, a fake life gives them courage and strength to face the outside world.

This might accurately embody how, nowadays, young people struggle to be accepted and feel like they have to rely on the Internet to get their needed recognition. It is said that "we are cultivating a generation of narcissists," but it is both unhelpful and obnoxious to shove aside a whole generation worth of worries, uncertainties, and reservations as something as simple as narcissism.

Elders often criticize them for being petty, weak, or even mentally unstable. And well, a lot of them credit their parents' trauma and toxic environment as the main reasons for therapeutic and psychological follow-ups.

Is the GenZ generation really to blame?

Or did this problem, this constant hunger for attention, start with the millennials?

The Eradication of Humanity
By Social Media

The millennials who are all so thirsty for Instagram fame that this transitioned into GenZ's addiction for TikTok.

Remember, Instagram launched in 2010. This was just two years after the financial crisis that shook us to our core and had worldwide ramifications. Some people lost everything—houses sat empty, many bankruptcies were declared, and once-safe assets shriveled up like raisins. In this scary and hopeless landscape, along came a little app called "Instagram," where beautiful photography reigned, and we could forget our worries.

Millennials, in particular, who had become disillusioned by the chaos surrounding them, found solace in this online world. We could post pictures of our dinners, adventures, and pets. It didn't matter that rent was due or that unemployment in the U.S. reached a high of 10%. For a brief moment, we could escape. As the number of friends on the app grew, so did our hunger for attention. If our following got bigger, all the better.

But these issues were hatched before they were even born; they didn't choose to face or experience them. If anything, it is a good thing that many are finally getting the help they need, motivating others to do the same. Even if it wasn't difficult or almost taboo to express oneself and one's passion, the times have changed and evolved. These highly influenceable young adults have struggled for years while trying to find themselves, their identity, the perfect job, or their happiness, and most did not seem to succeed.

People do not feel connected to their own lives and the people around them anymore. They feel lonely and abandoned by their own kin.

Yet, everyone needs others to rely on and to confide in. Everyone needs to feel the bond. So, they try, in whatever way they can, to connect themselves with others, even if it means talking and connecting with strangers. It is quite a contradictory behavior, as most of these same people suffer from interpersonal problems and avoid being physically present in social lives with friends or acquaintances. They feel rejected, unaccepted, and shamed for what they truly are. It is soothing to see people in the same situation or sharing the same experiences that bring them closer. But is this a real solution, or just temporary accommodations to delay fate?

Chapter Nine

How to Become TikTok Famous?

Let's broach the biggest question of all: how do we become TikTok famous? Unfortunately, there isn't a magical pill to swallow. No quick fix. Getting to the level of influencer stardom requires dedication and hard work. It requires years and years of specialized training. To be TikTok famous, you have to agree to be your most authentic and vulnerable self, make genuine connections with others, and most important of all, be humble.

If that sounds like a load of trash, congratulations! You caught us. To be TikTok famous, you don't need to do any of those things. Getting famous quick is as easy as A, B, C, so long as you're willing to do some basic research on algorithms, buy followers, and pander vain content to the masses. Many influencers have even written books on how to be Internet famous, such as Trisha Paytas telling her readers to sexualize themselves for fame.

TikTok stars, much like any other influencers who attract viewers, get the most traffic and make their videos stand out amongst the saturated crowd. They have endless video feeds that take them hours to create and edit before they finally post. Inexperienced users may believe that just posting is enough, and the rest is due to luck. They may think others are born to be influencer-material just because of their good looks, wealth, and better timing, but it isn't that simple.

None of it is done randomly or arbitrarily. Virtual assistants and marketing managers are key positions and occupational jobs that are in high demand. They require a proficient understanding of how to get the best out of investments, advertisements, or products. We all like to pretend our videos and posts are unfiltered and all-natural when they're clearly heavily edited and fake.

Why do we do this?

Why do we pretend to be angels on social media and act like complete assholes in reality?

Sooner or later, karma is going to bite us in the ass and return the favor.

The Eradication of Humanity
By Social Media

This karma sometimes comes in the form of reputation damage. Everything on the Internet is permanent. Even after deleting a picture or video, it technically still exists 1) in people's memories, and 2) in any saved, downloaded, or copied content. What happens when our future boss finds our inappropriate TikTok accounts? How will our future spouses feel when they look at our Facebook profiles and see the good, the bad, and the ugly?

The thing about posting our lives on social media is that we don't have a fair chance to defend ourselves from public misinterpretation. The embarrassing dance you did two years ago might turn off a potential employer who is hiring. The curse-filled political rant you engaged in on Instagram could really mess up how a new boyfriend or girlfriend views your potential as a partner. Since algorithms favor the bold, we are constantly pushing the limits of private information and what will connect with viewers and get us more followers, hearts, and likes. Risking our reputation is just one example.

We use premade and well-thought strategies to maximize the reach and conversion rate of these ads, while finding other less expensive but equally effective alternatives. We profit from how the algorithms were intended to work, knowing them inside out and using their knowledge to the advantage of the institution they work for.

We, as individuals, are crucial in the development of a good marketing and sales strategy for a company seeking to use social networks to both grow and expand its influence in the market. For entrepreneurs or individuals who are just starting out and cannot afford these services, we need to improvise.

TikTok's algorithm is mysterious. As an app, it is constantly growing and evolving, like some robotic cyborg straight out of a sci-fi movie. As TikTok changes over time, so does the algorithm. Social media strategists and users alike have been trying to figure out what exactly it takes to win the algorithm's favor. Articles abound on how to "beat" the algorithm. Here's what we know for sure.

First, we need to think about a thing called "video completion rate." This is how likely a viewer is to watch a TikTok video all the way to the end. The algorithm favors videos that hold user's attention spans, short as they are. As a reward for getting people to spend more time on their app, TikTok will show your video to a bigger audience if it is captivating enough. So, post short, catchy content, and your chances of going viral increase.

Secondly, we need to use good hashtags and write solid captions. Remember, TikTok only gives us a short space to express our thoughts. Write something that encourages people to comment, and the algorithm will push it for more engagement.

Lastly, and this should be obvious, only post high-quality videos. Add a beauty filter. Pick the perfect background music. If you want to please the algorithm, this is a must.

To become online famous, we need to make sure that our content is available and easy to find by using the right set of keywords that correspond to our account's identity. For example, let's dive into Instagram. Getting famous on this platform has become harder, but it isn't impossible. Sure, we could do the usual things—post consistently, have a theme, and schedule our grids in advance.

But that takes time and effort. We want results, and we want them now! For those of us who have money to burn, we buy followers. For as low as $10, we can go to a plethora of websites, like GrowthSilo, StormLikes, and Viralyft, and buy thousands of bot followers at a low cost. Some sites claim that we can purchase real followers, but most websites dedicated to selling fake followers give us bots or inactive accounts. So, what if our Instagram followers' number is 10,000? If 9,999 of those aren't real people, what did we really accomplish? Not much, we'd argue, except maybe an ego boost.

Brands looking to collaborate with big accounts also check engagement levels, as well as plain old numbers. If we have tons of followers, but they never comment on our pictures, we'd be better off building ourselves up organically. The only valid reason to buy followers on Instagram is for the bragging rights.

TikTok works a little bit differently, but there are still a certain number of methods to emphasize and increase its visibility. Many influencers, mostly on Instagram, apply several of these strategies every day. Some were shared by virtual assistants of influencers in hopes of helping people develop their brands and their identities on the Internet.

One of the shadiest practices used by people trying to grow their TikTok accounts is the act of buying followers, similar to Instagram. Keep in mind – TikTok is not a charity. It is a moneymaking platform. There is serious cash to be made if people are willing to use unscrupulous means to get there. Even small accounts with 1,500 followers have the chance to monetize. And the earnings are unlimited.

So, how do we do it? How do we go from being a "nobody" with a real-life friend count of maybe fifteen to an influencer god? Easy. We empty our bank accounts.

Step One: Be desperate. Organic growth can take months, sometimes years. We don't have time for that. Instead, we head on over to websites like TikTokPalace, where, for $45, we can purchase 2,500 new followers.

Step Two: Bribe other accounts. Offering to send someone a "gift" or fee in exchange for giving our TikTok page a shout-out is a surefire way to get a dozen or so new fans. This tactic works well for those with something to offer, say, a free copy of our book or a custom piece of artwork. But at the end of the day, money is king.

TikTok bots are another option. Totally unregulated, bots allow us to interact with other accounts without ever actually lifting a finger. This can include fake comments, likes, emojis on videos, and anything that will generate traffic and heighten our chances of gaining followers. For instance, FuelTok charges $29 per month to "growth hack" an account. This software guarantees reliable growth. They even offer a 7-day free trial to get us hooked on the service.

And lastly, we can post despairing content. These days, it seems like every new account posts at least one "woe is me" style clip of themselves bemoaning the fact that they only have ten followers. Nobody likes me; I have no friends; I'm so sad. We pull at heartstrings, gain their sympathy, and boom! Hundreds of new followers.

In each of our interactions with our audience, we apply these tactics to boost and enhance our presence online. The chances are slim, but some of us have sought to understand more about TikTok's algorithm in hopes of improving them. As on all social networking platforms, the latter is governed by predefined criteria, which it uses to process and analyze videos, thus deciding what percentage of individuals it will be exposed to. Suppose it does well with a slim percentage of individuals, soliciting them into liking, sharing, or commenting. In that case, the algorithm deems it worthy of being presented to a bigger share of potential new followers.

If used to a TikToker's advantage, this processing data can sometimes make a big difference of several thousand views. Underdeveloped at the moment, it still needs much improvement and users' experiences to correct potential operating errors and improve its standards to give a fighting chance to all those who actually produce good content.

However, it also confronts creators with choosing their content, not based on their personal tastes or even their current goals, but solely based on what the algorithm favors. Their uniqueness and fun personality, which people originally loved them for, are engulfed by the expectations and desire to get more and more followers. This forces creators to make popular content instead of focusing on making content they love—always seeing into the future, without valuing the present.

This very fact becomes frustrating as our personal freedom is robbed from us, as our success is not equivalent to the efforts we put into the content. Instead, it's determined by whether what we produce is algorithm-friendly or not. It gives certain people advantages, which is the definition of favoritism and, by extension, prejudice.

The challenges mentioned previously are part of the actual trends that TikTok encourages its creators to try to surf in so they can catch the wave. They are not obliged to do so, but isn't it so tempting? We almost become forced to join the crowds of social media that we once abhorred, or risk becoming socially isolated and dejected.

People have become so obsessed with having everything online that they find it difficult to escape.

Some of the criteria noted above, which could turn out to be mere conjecture, include dancing, using popular songs or filters, surfing on popular trends or challenges, posting videos half-naked, being beautiful, smiling, adding captions or hashtags, and talking about social or political issues. Users of the platform have come to a consensus as to the benefit that exploiting these requirements provides, most having experienced first-hand through several videos put together back-to-back that they really do not share the same success.

Posted in intervals of only a few seconds, those who correspond to the favored patterns manifest four to five times the amount of views of those who don't. It is obvious that TikTok's algorithm has to be based on something. It has to rely on pre-established settings to function. Some of them are acceptable, others are not, given that the algorithm encourages users to expose their bodies and skin for a larger viewership.

Social media such as Instagram, TikTok, and YouTube has made it all too easy for us to become famous. But at what cost? With how easy it is for us to quickly become a somebody, it's that same quickness that can cause us to fall and become a nobody. Unless we become famous through sheer talent rather than just a viral video of our mental breakdowns, we are bound to be forgotten. And then what?

The Internet creates us; it can take it all away within a matter of seconds. Take, for example, the tragic death of 22-year-old YouTube sensation Christina Grimmie, whose life was taken away too soon by an obsessed fan who found her on the Internet and wanted nothing more than to be with her...in life or in death. The Internet is a fueling platform for stalkers and sociopaths, who target famous people online and claim them for themselves with their delusion.

The amount of followers has become a way to measure our importance.

Why?

What does a counter say about our self-worth?

What does it say about how pretty or intelligent we are?

Why must people get stuck on these figures, never satisfied or fulfilled by the fame it has brought them already?

A huge count of followers will never be able to replace family and friends that we need in real life.

The Eradication of Humanity
By Social Media

Why base self-empathy, pity, love, and esteem on a fleeting, precarious, and ever-so-changing number that relies on people's whimsical feelings of affection towards an Internet and social media persona they have only seen from the other side of a screen?

Several arguments come to mind. First of all, an audience shares an appreciation for the content creator. Whether it is out of egocentricity, narcissism, or simply the lack of recognition and affection mentioned earlier, the creator seeks feedback, smiles, compliments, or a little bit of everything from the audience. As it would for singers, the latter will grant people the applause they need to reassure themselves that they're great.

All to make the hours spent in a studio or in front of a screen editing a 60-second video worthwhile.

To prove to themselves that they matter and that they are not useless.

To give them strength to continue pursuing their dreams.

Because someone is backing them up, nurturing them as they go, and that is all the support they need.

This applause will reward all the hours lost thinking about new themes, writing a script, or buying props to use. It is also important to understand that the number of followers is often associated with quality. As the number of followers increases, it is widely assumed that the quality of the content also increases. Or at least that they are equivalent to one another. However, that's not always the case. Users themselves will be more inclined to subscribe to a content creator who is already recognized by a large community, regardless of their content. An influencer with a million followers can easily produce poor material, and people will still follow and subscribe.

The Eradication of Humanity
By Social Media

But it's our fault that influencers have become out of control. We feed into their habits by encouraging them to do more despite the content being toxic to both themselves and their viewers. The more we pay attention to them, the more they are likely to create similar content. Take YouTuber Eugenia Cooney, for example. The more attention viewers give to her, expressing concerns over her Anorexic tendencies, the more she's likely to continue, using comments as fuel because they give her attention. Even if we hate someone on the Internet and what they stand for or do, the more attention we give to them, the more likely they are to continue.

Sometimes we even follow those with content we're not even sure we like, only because they already have a vast amount of followers.

Nowhere is this better exemplified than on Instagram. In addition to buying followers, another tactic used to gain a massive following in a short period of time is the so-called "follow/unfollow" method. What we do is this: find accounts similar to ours. Then, we go on a rampage where we hit the follow button on every single account that is in the same niche as our own. For example, if we have a fashion account, we seek out #fashionista. Great!

Now, because Instagram depends on engagement and interactions to be successful, lots of times, the people we follow will follow us back. We wait until they do so, and then BAM! We unfollow them. It's a well-known desire among all wannabe influencers to want to appear like they have a ton of followers without following a lot themselves. That gives them the appearance that they finally made it as true celebrities, despite knocking a couple thousand people down along the way.

We don't care about these accounts. Hell, we might not even have an interest in them at all. It doesn't matter. All that matters is that we tricked others into returning our follow, and now, we've falsely inflated our numbers to look more popular than we actually are. It's a proven strategy, one that works well for tiny creators who are too lazy to grow their accounts organically.

Deceitful?

Absolutely.

But it's effective.

As vulnerable human beings, we feel this drive to walk towards where the crowd already is, even if we have no idea what the destination is. Why? Because we have an inherent need to belong, to feel sociable, even when we know we don't belong.

Chapter Ten

How Much Does It Cost to Sabotage Our Own Lives?

Something that shouldn't come as a surprise to most is that many social networking platforms are monetized. Therefore, having more followers means more money and more compensation for the creative account. This definitely motivates young and lazy hopefuls to try and make a living off the Internet to avoid getting an actual job. It's great to see that expensive education being put to good use on viral challenge videos that land people in the hospital.

Are these materialistic people, whose only concern is to make the most of their creative profiles, or are they just tired of the normal 9 to 5 and have found a better way to generate income while staying in bed? Monetization and sponsorships from content have decreased the integrity people used to have for honest, hard-working jobs, now turning to stripping and putting their lives in danger's way to get paid.

Hint: you can't spend that money if you're dead!

However, this is the case for a small handful. Those with a few million subscribers could already use this influencer activity as their main source of income and devote themselves entirely to their passion. It's not easy to say exactly how much money this brings. TikTok has reported that for every one thousand views, the usual amount paid is fixed between two and four dollars. That isn't much, but since TikTok brews a lot of content, these creators' videos can easily reach one hundred thousand views. If you add to this the commercial communications or product placements for which they are paid much more (this can be as much as $10 or $20 per thousand views), you can estimate a creator's earnings for a single video to be over $20,000. That's crazy money for people who spend less than an hour a day creating content!

Let's look at YouTube. American YouTuber and cosmetics guru, Jeffree Star, brings in about 200 million per year off his channel. This includes affiliates, endorsement deals, and brand sponsorships, but what has really helped this Internet celebrity cash in isn't his makeup talent alone – it's his ability to respond to trash talk.

Naturally, seeing creators get rich makes others jealous. Lots of other creators have "come for" Jeffree Star to throw shade, bring him down, and get his account demonetized. On YouTube and TikTok, people post rude videos about him, his ex, his dogs...anything to draw attention off Star and onto themselves. Quite brilliantly, Jeffree Star, in turn, uses this fuel to burn his own fire hotter.

In a YouTube video titled, "Reacting to MEAN TikToks About Me (This Crossed The Line!)," Star shares his responses to all the hate while stirring the pot further. The end result? Even more attention! The hateful videos meant to demonetize the influencer backfired. But that doesn't stop people from trying; millions of dollars are at stake. Some of us will do whatever it takes to get a piece of the pie.

Of course, this is only a rough estimate, based on monetization data that must surely be adapted to the type of content and even the length of the video. So, it's not a sure thing. But these days, it's a serious career that can have many advantages. Nevertheless, we need to be confident in our own abilities, because the slightest mistake, the slightest false gesture, can lead to the collapse of an entire life project with serious repercussions on our mental and financial health. While many are able to retire early with their vast earnings on social media, being a full-time influencer doesn't last long and cannot be considered a long-lasting career by any means. The Internet is what creates these people, and the Internet is what can tear them all down.

Older generations often criticize and discount this tendency that new generations have to turn towards social media and startup positions instead of pursuing their education and occupying traditional work professions. They would rather live an unstable and unreliable lifestyle through photoshoots, filming, and streaming rather than work normal full-time jobs. However, this is understandable, since employment was once seen as a secure occupation to obtain money and afford the high costs of living in society.

The Eradication of Humanity
By Social Media

Many people reluctantly had to take on physically or mentally demanding work, which they rarely enjoyed due to the difficult conditions they were in. Since it was their only source of income, they continued to do so until retirement, hoping to have enough, though many still don't. Today, things have changed. Nevertheless, despite the content people create online, cancel culture has taken a huge toll on people's incomes, canceling creators left and right for content they don't subjectively agree with.

New generations can afford to choose their next job based on their preferences and talents, whereas previous generations used to be forced to take whatever job will hire them. This new generation has what, for most people, would've been a luxury at the time. For most, they can take the time for education and training, which was not the case before. We even see people busking and begging for money despite them not actually being homeless, seeing this as an "easy profession."

Now, we don't know everyone's unique situation. We don't know what goes on behind closed doors. But what is undeniable is that there are two viral trends growing at an alarming rate. First, film yourself donating money to a homeless individual, thus portraying yourself as a hero and getting a nice ego boost at the same time. And second, pretend to be homeless yourself. Obviously, both issues present substantial moral dilemmas.

Take @cobypersin, for example. He films social experiments where he pretends to be homeless to see how people will react to his plight. Played over sad piano music, he records total strangers and asks them for money. When a generous woman (who is homeless herself) donates a few dollars, he immediately jumps up and explains that this was a trick to see what people would do. At first, we think of this as an educational video. Wow! Look at how horrible people are. Look how kind that woman who has nothing is. We all need to do better.

The Eradication of Humanity
By Social Media

Dig a little deeper, and this man's actions are highly problematic. Rather than getting at the root causes of homelessness (high housing costs, addictions, lack of mental health services, gaps in education, low-income jobs, etc.), @cobypersin reduces the issue of homelessness down to a 20-second clip. Yes, he is raising awareness. 1.6 million people "liked" his video. It's meant to be heartwarming.

But who did he actually help?

What's the point of awareness if no actual change takes place?

How many of us will now go out and volunteer in a soup kitchen or press our politicians for immediate social change?

How many of us will become homelessness advocates for those less fortunate?

In reality, we will smile, double-tap the video to show our approval of his good deed, and move on with our days.

For Twitch streamers, it's a different story. Unlike the example above, which seeks out attention for a (false) good deed, streamers on Twitch aren't grinding for the attention...they're after the money.

Some Twitch streamers have figured out a way to turn their content into a full-time job. Richard Blevins, or Ninja, accumulates a respectable 5.4 million per year. On Reddit, there is a post titled, "Any full-time/part-time streamer that works a full-time job? What's it like?" Here, we can see how, at 40 hours per week, for between 2-5 streams that go on for multiple hours, Twitch gamers are pulling in decent money.

Neither physically nor mentally demanding, it's great income for those willing to be locked to their screens. One commenter shared, "If you plan to do this, keep in mind that you'll get very little sleep." Disrupted sleep patterns, sore backs, muscle cramps in the hands, and heightened stress levels are all common for diehard gamers.

Despite the drawbacks, we see new creators pop up all the time who make a higher income off of streaming than if they had an ordinary 9-5 job. According to Business of Apps, the average full-time streamer can expect to make between $3,000 to $5,000 a month. Just playing video games! That's crazy good money compared to a minimum wage job. No wonder so many people want in.

The world is constantly changing and developing every day towards a future where new technologies make human comfort a precious commodity. Everything is invented and realized to make daily life easier and more accessible. As a matter of fact, many jobs transformed, whilst others disappeared. Many became easier to accomplish, thanks to the computerization of tasks and the use of machines for many stages of construction.

The future isn't guaranteed, so what will become of younger generations when social media becomes a thing of the past? Unlike past generations, we don't have scrapbooks filled with black and white photographs, or boxes stashed away in the attic stuffed to the brim with old mementos. Instead, our lives are fossilized online. When TikTok dies, or fades away as it gets replaced with a newer, hipper social media, what will happen to our sense of self?

Likely, we will feel lost. Our identities are so wrapped up in these 30-second clips that we have neglected real-life friendships and family relationships. When it all comes crashing down, we just have to wonder if younger generations will have the coping skills to deal with this identity crisis.

The new generation has indeed taken too much for granted, which makes older generations' worries relatable. Social media makes everything look far too easy. As anyone can become the next Internet phenomenon, there is always the will to take a chance at becoming a coveted celebrity. Who would resist taking an open door if it could lead them to a life of financial stability and permanent admiration from their community? Almost no one would deny the benefits that such visibility and social presence bring. Many of them are recovering, getting their senses together, or trying to achieve this goal while holding one or more small part-time jobs on the side.

In the end, it's like playing the lottery. Humans hope to win the substantial amount that is promised, and they're ready to spend money every time for a new ticket that has infinitesimal chances of being the one. Why do they still chase this impossible dream? Because it would relieve their monotonous lives and their constant struggles for money sufficiency.

How we make a living has changed forever. Like when the industrial revolution hit, we are now in a transition period, where the information age and the entertainment age overlap. Wealth disparity is at an all-time high—the poor are getting poorer, and the ultra-rich are getting richer. For most of us, a comfortable life is the goal. Sure, 9-5 office jobs still exist. But they are getting harder to come by. And we don't have the attention spans to sit in front of a computer all day long doing monotonous work. So, then what?

Well, we all have phones. For the first time in history, the playing field has been leveled in the sense that, as long as we have Internet access and a phone, we have just as much of a shot as anybody else in making it big. For those of us yearning for financial security, the idea is tempting.

But using social media as the only form of income is not necessarily out of selfishness or vanity. Maybe those who made it big are the ones who started off using it just as a hobby, seeing nothing more to it until something blew up. And then when sponsorships and fans started coming in, it became difficult to step out of the spotlight even if they wanted to, feeling pressured to create and post content similar to the ones that made them famous, or else they lose all of it and become the next joke on YouTube.

While it's true that many teens and young adults ruin their lives by becoming far too preoccupied with appearances and social networks, chasing after an unreachable dream and putting themselves through never-ending torture, never realizing that it's a lost cause until it's too late, there are also those who struggle to just be an average person again. With Internet fame, comes a lot of risk. People will always try to expose you or hurt you, and it's a struggle for some to keep up with the crowd.

Although I'm not an advocate of spending thousands of dollars on an education that can potentially lead to nowhere, when we solely focus on becoming Internet famous, we're putting ourselves at greater risk for homelessness and failure than if we were to get that degree and take even a minimal wage job. There are some people who put all their eggs in one basket, so convinced that they are going to become Internet famous, that they resort to putting their lives in danger or completely embarrassing themselves to get that little bit of attention.

We live in a culture where we think anything is achievable, so we give up stable income and chase after quick and easy money. We underestimate how much work and how many years it takes to become Internet famous. Not all of us can be lucky enough to have one viral video blow up and give us millions of dollars.

Those who become rich and famous online, those who really make it, are people who spend hours and hours on creating visually appealing content, marketing, editing, designing merch, and spending gruesome hours developing a following. They never stop working on their material because they know that once they stop, they lose it all.

But most people don't know this. Most believe that only creating videos or only taking pictures will get them to their dream goal. People get tired and bored very easily. Internet creators are forced to change and expand their content even if they don't completely stand by the modifications, just to please their new followers and keep the old ones from leaving. They spend so much time pleasing others that you begin to wonder if content creators are still doing what they love for themselves.

When creators have a following, a truly loyal following, it almost doesn't matter what they do anymore, as long as they're constantly surprising their fans and remaining unpredictable. This already puts them a step ahead of their competitors, who have to base their commercial and advertising strategies on much more impersonal elements, which often won't reach their entire target audience. Some examples include Kanye West, who decided to run for president while many analysts feared that, with his worldwide popularity, he would be elected, despite the fact that he lacked the qualifications for the position. Another example is Squeezie, a French Youtuber who won the NRJ Music Awards with an amateur song, even though his primary field of interest is gaming.

Many designers on TikTok have already taken advantage of their audience to launch authentic clothing brands or handmade stores that they also share on their videos. Instead of reacting like many viewers on the YouTube platform (outraged that designers use them for their commercial communications and product placements), the audience on TikTok seems to react positively to the products they can acquire from their favorite designers at lower prices. We could also say that the latter takes advantage of their followers to make money more easily, pushing them to buy their products, but how do we know what's really going on? It depends entirely on the point of view adopted. Isn't that right?

Chapter Eleven

Privacy Breach

However, what would happen to these creators who gain fame at any cost on the Internet through viral posts when TikTok or other social platforms no longer exists? As surprising as it may sound, the likelihood of this happening is real, all too real. Many platforms, aside from the giants, are only around for a few years before disappearing, as the labor and operating costs of such a high-scale organization are outrageous. Networks providing similar features tend to go through a natural filtering process, usually until one remains that has managed to gather more users and larger support from the public. Twitch and Mixer could serve as the main examples for this concept, as the latter spent too much trying to rival the already implemented giant which dominated the market, even though it had Microsoft's backing.

As of recent events, TikTok was almost banned from the United States via the initiative and decision of former President Donald Trump, under both assumptions and suspicions of an underlying clandestine use of confidential and private information of the app's users by the Chinese corporation, ByteDance.

One thing we know for sure is that personal information belonging to TikTok users was breached.

The true extent of the damage is still a mystery. But what happened was the horrors of every parent's nightmare. A seemingly harmless app downloaded by their child was suddenly streaming on every news station across America – and not for good reasons. ByteDance, a Chinese owned company, was accused of collaborating with the Chinese Communist Party (CCP) to steal user information and omit consent practices. Worst of all? Their main targets were children.

Lawyers and politicians argued that TikTok "infiltrated its users' devices and extracted a broad array of private data." This included private biometric data such as face scans. This data was then sent to servers in China. Interesting to note that, in China, surveillance of citizens using such tactics is commonplace. Privacy laws are weak, and all companies that store data are subjected to government-conducted security checks. To think that the Chinese government would not be heavily involved in globally popular apps, such as TikTok, would be naïve.

Lawyers fighting against TikTok also said that the app was used to "track and profile TikTok users for the purpose of, among other things, targeting and profit." Essentially, no effort was made to protect children's privacy. Add this to the fact that minors do not yet possess the brainpower to read and understand all the fine print before downloading an app, and we have a recipe for disaster.

Obviously, privacy isn't just a U.S. concern. On June 29, 2020, the Indian government made the bold move of banning TikTok. Why? Same deal—alleged national security issues. This is not the first time this developing country has tried to ban the application, but this time, it succeeded. They've used data protection concerns as a pretext like the United States did, and there is no way to know in whose mind the idea spurred first. What can be said is that this is just one more step in the economic war that India and China have been waging in for a long time.

But ByteDance is one of the most valuable technology companies in the world. They were not going to give up so easily. After all, the former President had planned to ban it everywhere on American territory! While the case settled (for now), it amounts to proving that, even though the end of TikTok may not be near, the dangers regarding its guaranteed access remain a fear in us all.

ByteDance, surely out of fear of losing a large part of its customers and its presence on the western market, has accepted many changes in its policies, while trying to find an amiable end to all the controversy. They wanted to ensure that the fears expressed by the politician were unfounded. Thus, they appointed an American corporate director, who took charge of managing the American branch. Although the head office will still be located in Beijing, this creates a false sense of security in the minds of Americans.

The Eradication of Humanity
By Social Media

Facebook faces similar challenges with regards to the safe storage of data. With Facebook, there are two aspects to consider. First, is small-time identity theft. Second, is largescale data hacking, as we covered earlier. In both cases, the consequences can be serious.

The whole point of Facebook is to connect. To do this, we have to give birth to an online representation of ourselves that is accurate and highlights the best version of who we are. That means we need to share intimate details of our lives, the things we are most proud of, and what makes us look good in the eyes of others. So, we upload family photo albums.

We add where we graduated high school or college in our bios. To feel like we belong to part of a team, we also search for our coworkers' names and make private group chats. We add our birthdays because – duh! Who doesn't want to receive a hundred Happy Birthday wishes over the Internet? The absurdity of how much information we post knows no limits. After having babies and before we've even left the hospital, we upload newborn announcements to Facebook so that everybody can see how special we are, how much we deserve to be loved and celebrated.

And what's the harm? It's only friends and family seeing this stuff, right? Wrong.

Devious players with dubious intents comb through accounts every day, looking for weaknesses in privacy protection. Usually, money is the driving force. Victims of identity theft on Facebook might be asked for ransom money in exchange for getting their accounts back into their hands. Or, their friends may be fed lies about financial struggles of another friend and unknowingly send e-transfers to who they think is their friend but is actually an imposter. It's the classic "Nigerian Prince" scam but adapted for the twenty-first century.

The Eradication of Humanity
By Social Media

These days, it's easy enough to guess or hack a password, or take advantage of someone who didn't fully log out of their account on, say, a library computer, for example. In fact, identity theft is so common on Facebook that there is a "How to report identity theft on Facebook" section on their help page.

In 2018, CBS ran a story about identity scams on Facebook. Turns out, roughly $220 million went missing, thanks to similar con artist Internet scams. Just look at singer Justin Bieber. His legitimate account has a blue checkmark. But that hasn't stopped dozens of fake accounts claiming to be him from popping up and trying to "sell" tickets to naïve users.

We can fault Facebook for failing to guard our data against hostile foreign entities. But when we put up photos of our kids, our houses, workplaces, and all the teeny tiny details of our lives, who do we really have to blame but ourselves when a scammer comes sniffing around for an easy win?

Many of us see losing our accounts as devastating, whether it's because our social media platform got shut down or because our identity was stolen.

As for now, talks about TikTok have ceased, and creators can finally sleep at night knowing that they will still be able to access their accounts and reach their hard-earned followers the next morning. But it's not like they were ready to go down without a fight, many having invited their current followers to join them on another platform they had prepared beforehand so as to not lose them.

Luckily, creators fearing the worst had many platforms to choose from. Instagram proved popular. Many creators posted TikTok videos saying goodbye, in case that was the last time they were able to interact with their fans before the shutdown. At the end of their clips, they tagged their Instagram handles and invited followers to migrate over. Some did. But the void TikTok would leave behind if it did get banned would be massive. For diehard TikTokers, the "Stories" reel on the 'gram feels too fake, too shallow. Plus, it's old—by social media standards, practically ancient.

Enter Clubhouse. Initially released in April 2020, this app is a fresh take on audio technology. Basically, it's a chatroom. No photos, videos, or even text. For those seeking a new platform to whisk away their followers to, Clubhouse was a popular choice at the time. The biggest downside? It's invitation only. That means exclusivity. For some, this adds to the appeal. But for users who just want a new space to hang out, TikTok is still the superior app.

Keep in mind, TikTok is much more than just an application for many people all over the world. In India, TikTok was like a breath of fresh air in a country so affected by poverty. Poverty afflicts more than half of the population, and illiteracy is at more than 25%. The application's video-based content allowed anyone with a cell phone, even an old model, to enjoy it. As most people do not own laptops and rely solely on their phones to connect or surf the Internet, the app was assured of its success. It was an escape from censorship, discrimination, and the caste system that represses them. It transcended castes, religions, and other social fractures that the country is going through.

Everybody was in the same boat. In a country where their lack of power and influence have long silenced the poor, TikTok was a place to express themselves without worrying about the repercussions. All is not rosy, though, because while the application gave a voice to many young people and motivated mobilizations (demonstrations, awareness-raising, and social organization), it also showcased abusive sexual content and misinformation of messages. This raised legitimate concerns about the use of the platform in the already unstable country of India. Adolescents were posting disturbing and traumatic videos featuring suicides and even acid attacks.

Chapter Twelve

Is It Really Worth It?

What could be a more effective way to prove the distress in which the population of this country is plunged, for whom TikTok was finally a drug that gave them courage and pushed them to a possible reversal of the pre-established trend in their own country?

The Eradication of Humanity
By Social Media

Believing that the permanent ban of TikTok in America could have saved people from addiction and all the darkness underlying the platform, rather than leaving them to their fate, proves to be a very naive and wishful way of thinking. People would still find a way to create content.

India can most certainly prove it. Similar apps experienced a sudden rise in numbers as soon as TikTok was taken out. If there is no existing competitor to replace it in the people's hearts, there soon will be. Instagram Reels and Chingari are the main suitors, but there could always be another app currently in a rushed development, hoping to occupy the gap left in the country.

Certainly, TikTok shows a lot of potential and is well-loved, but it is still a means to an end regardless of the country. Despite the inherent disappointment and attachment that these creators may have had to their former community and content, there is nothing to stop them from starting anew elsewhere, without forgetting to urge their followers to join and follow them. Indeed, it represents a huge loss for them, several million for some Indian influencers.

But there will always be another way. People will always strive to find another social media where they can share the same experiences. So, all in all, they are just waiting for a future TikTok-like app to reveal itself. Everything is bound to be replaced.

And TikTok's long-term fame, which all apps aspire to, is not only hard to obtain; it is almost impossible. It is a pretty illusion, like many others use to lure in new gullible and easy-going individuals that will be part of their showcase to attract new users to their platform. They will be nothing more than a tool for the application, shimmering with illusory gains that will never be attributed to them. And only very rarely will they be able to provide the content and the possibility to go viral necessary to reach this coveted celebrity status.

The Eradication of Humanity
By Social Media

But even if it does work out, even if they do attain the hard-earned fame, it can come crashing down in an instant if the app was to ever disappear or get banned from the country they originated from, leaving the people with nothing. Imagine spending years dedicated to one platform, one thing, just to have it all disappear in the blink of an eye. Many would have no choice but to start over, like the examples aforementioned, once again in another social media network, where nothing would be the same, counting on the few followers they manage to bring along...

But it does raise a few conflicting questions.

Was it really worth it?

Were all their efforts not in vain after all?

Did they accomplish very little despite wasting hundreds of hours of their precious time to build a virtual structure that, in the end, can collapse effortlessly?

Or is there another motive behind this presence on the Internet that explains, in their eyes, all the trouble they went through?

TikTok is a trap. It's like a gaping hole into which one falls and then has trouble crawling out of. It's a bottomless well, and sometimes, you don't even notice the fall. It's easy to get a few tens of thousands of followers in the beginning. The first stage is by far the easiest to cross. But what next?

Are we willing to invest all the effort needed to take the next step?

Are we going to be satisfied and take advantage of what we've learned, which may soon be lost, especially if it all started with a single viral video?

The Eradication of Humanity
By Social Media

Will we give up everything, our success being entirely due to a sudden rush, pure adrenaline, and a passing curiosity?

Is it enough to be popular on TikTok?

If the passing of time doesn't take care of eliminating some creators who are too unmotivated to keep up, TikTok will take charge in lifting the heat off them.

Maybe that's why they decide to shadowban, randomly or not, some creators on their platform.

So that the latter stop growing and chaining the millions of views, which will have to be paid for, or would it be to test them to see how far they are willing to go?

How do we find out?

There are two ways to destroy an influencer: shadowban or cancel them. We see it happen all the time. One day, we are scrolling through posts by our favorite accounts—sometimes multiple per day—then, all of a sudden, they seemingly disappear. Where did the person go? Did they delete their account? We search for their names and are able to find them. How odd, we think. It's almost as if somebody was purposely blocking their content from reaching our eyes.

Bingo. That's exactly how it goes down. Content is either fully or partially concealed from the public under a practice called "Shadowbanning." This can include video footages, images, comments, likes, etc. In some cases, a shadowban can be useful. Troll or spammer accounts that get shadowbanned eventually tend to go away. Some people with problematic content, who find themselves without a following, will often delete their accounts and leave in favor of another platform (though, more likely than not, they'll just make a secondary account under a new name).

The Eradication of Humanity
By Social Media

But what about ordinary users?

How do we know if we've been the victim of a shadowban?

Well, engagement will be lower. Shadowbans are effective because they stop connections from being made. If you're used to getting a couple hundred "likes" on a video but now only get one or two, chances that your account has been targeted are high.

For example, look at popular cosplayer, Tanya. She goes by @shinorisu on TikTok. Recently, she shared an "important update" video in which she explained that her account had been banned for repeated warnings. With no details given, she is left wondering what exactly she did to upset the TikToks gods. Subsequently, she is now likely shadowbanned. While her followers can still search for her, new accounts won't see her promoted on their "For You Page." Thus, she is missing out on a huge demographic moving forward.

It's not always done with nefarious intent, however. Every now and again, a hashtag glitch will result in an unintended ban. These are almost always temporary. To be on the safe side, it's best practice to steer clear of posting too much "spammy" content, lest you fall prey to the dreaded shadowban also.

The second way to completely ruin a creator is to #cancel them. This method is not for the faint of heart. To be cancelled is to have all your friends, fans, and followers turn on you. It is the online version of boycotting. All support for a creator cease. Since they are famous, celebrities are usually targeted. For instance, in the year 2020, big names were cancelled—J.K. Rowling was accused of transphobia, Dr. Seuss was attacked for discrimination, and Ellen DeGeneres was the recipient of brutal backlash surrounding her poor treatment of talk show staffers.

The Eradication of Humanity
By Social Media

And let's not forget one of the most controversial of all – beauty influencer, James Charles. In just one weekend, he lost 3 million subscribers on YouTube. As quickly as he accumulated his fame, he lost it. A mass exodus of fans fled when scandal after scandal came to light, blaming Charles for ruining friendships and being fake.

Like the Olympics, we all tune in to watch an influencer burn in a blaze of cancel-culture glory. There's just something about watching the downfall of another that is addictive to social media users. As long as it is never us, we are happy to participate in the ruining of lives, whether the person deserves it or not.

Nobody exemplifies this better than Jenna Marbles. Once an adored Internet celebrity, loved for her quirky sense of humor, cute dogs, and funny videos, Marbles became the subject of intense Internet scrutiny. Like villagers with fiery pitchforks, she was chased off of YouTube. Why? Cancel culture.

The year was 2011. In a series of YouTube videos, Jenna Marbles joked about blackface and Asians. Fast-forward to the modern-day with cancel culture in full swing, Jenna Marbles became the target of those looking for someone – anyone – to make an example out of. For something she did ten years ago, she was "cancelled." Hateful messages were written in the comments section of her YouTube videos. She was talked about and debated on live television. Fans and enemies alike were in an uproar. For those of us who watched her show, it was the juiciest gossip around.

Ultimately, the pressure got to be too much. In a very emotional goodbye video, we watched Marbles apologize. She said she never intended to hurt people and promised to do better. Unfortunately, this wasn't good enough for the Internet goblins' intent on watching her burn. The situation got so bad that she left YouTube for good. The kicker? One stupid mistake a decade ago tarnished her career so badly that it might never fully recover. Because of an insensitive and, yes, problematic video, everyone suddenly forgot all the good Marbles did to promote kindness, body positivity, and dog rescue.

This is the effect of cancel culture. We demonize those we disagree with and to hell with their apologies! There is no room for growth and no chance at reconciliation. We only want to watch them fall. We shout for change, but we all know that's not what we want. We're jealous. We're out for blood.

YouTuber Gabbie Hanna summarized it this way: "Let's stop normalizing going back through ten years of somebody's life, hoping you stumble upon a mistake and try to ruin their life." What will happen when cancel culture gets so out of control, and nobody is left?

Either way, it is impossible to see the future. No one is endowed with such gifts, but human nature allows us to foresee that no one will ever be satisfied. It's in our nature to always want more, to always want the things we don't have, even when we don't know what that something is. It's stronger than we are. It is an instinct, something primitive and unconscious.

And at the same time, we find it normal. We are always trying to get more, whether it's fame, power, or love. Nothing is ever enough. So, we find ourselves chasing a goal we can never fully achieve. It's a follower's race that will always result in a new level of achievement. And if some always manage to stay in the race, others have to suffer and go through the filtering, the censorship, and the limitations of TikTok to even hope to make it.

Chapter Thirteen

Censored, Cancelled, and Banned. You're Next!

Despite all that has been said, TikTok is not a place where we can succeed without putting in an equivalent amount of work. As noted above, creators have recently started showing apprehension regarding the app's algorithm and their total viewership.

The Eradication of Humanity
By Social Media

They started experiencing the following: videos on which the fame counter would rise to half a million in a few hours suddenly struggled to make a thousand in a few days, several videos started getting taken down by TikTok with no plausible explanation, the traffic suddenly decreased, the number of interactions dropped in free fall, and the number of new followers shrunk with some even resorting to unsubscribing because they no longer see any new content from the creators' pages.

This decline is the worst nightmare of all creators. As mentioned previously, this phenomenon is called being "shadowbanned." This term applies to the considerable loss of viewership they experience because of it. Meaningless. As invisible as shadows. Banned from the platform without any crime or mistake to account for. It's like trying to run a race with a concrete ball chained to the ankle, and no one knows how to get rid of it.

No one knows where TikTok has hidden the keys. This is dangerous, especially in countries where people value freedom of speech and expression. Censoring can lead to fierce backlash and hate. Silencing people on one platform only increases their anger on another.

Earlier, we explored famous celebrities who had been shadowbanned. But be warned! This can happen to anyone, and it's not a TikTok-specific problem. YouTube vloggers, Instagram gurus, and Twitter tweeters have all been recipients of the much-feared shadowban.

And that's how we can begin to associate TikTok with a tyrant who holds all the power on the platform. The creators don't decide the reach or success of their videos. They simply post content they hope will be popular and well-received, then leave it to the algorithm and goodwill of TikTok, who then decides, by its own free will, what will become of that video. TikTok, like other social platforms, can choose to completely ban or remove certain content or videos without any notice, leaving creators to wonder whether it's even worth going through all that effort.

Creators sometimes try to fight back by calling out the app or posting angry videos about the degenerating condition of their profiles, but it doesn't seem to amount to anything other than shame and a loss of followers. In an attempt to break the trend, some creators try to post videos that they know are favored by the algorithm, siding with and promoting things they know people will want to hear, losing themselves in the process. Some theories support this being a good way to regain the algorithm's favor before returning to their usual content, but this hypothesis has never been confirmed.

As a result, people started feeling particularly anxious about being the next target because no one knows what triggers it. They just start noticing the consequences and try to figure it out. There is no way to turn it back—it is totally out of their control. Those who rely on TikTok for their main source of income, and store owners who count on their faithful followers for the success of their brand-new businesses, are by far the most affected. It usually doesn't last long, but let's imagine that it does.

What will become of these people?

Will they be compelled to beg their followers or the random viewers that come across their content to buy their products?

Will they need to quit TikTok and try their luck on another social media platform?

Will they resort to making dance videos and challenges instead of their usual content to stay visible?

What more do they need to remain in the good graces of TikTok?

The Eradication of Humanity
By Social Media

The problem is so pervasive that there are even articles on, "How to tell if you've been shadowbanned on social media." Facebook, Instagram, and TikTok seem to have the most claims of shadowbanning practices. Twitter takes a different approach. On their blog, Twitter explicitly states that they *do not* shadowban.

Instead, they tackle who they call "bad-faith actors." These are spammers, trolls, or people who seem inauthentic in some way (who exactly is responsible for determining these traits, we don't know). Rather than an outright ban, Twitter will rank posts lower. Less exposure means less engagement. It's a different strategy but has similar results.

If we thought that it couldn't get much worse, that TikTok had already taken away our privileges and our voices, that censoring was as bad as it was going to get, well, we were wrong. TikTok is a well-oiled machine whose gears work in perfect harmony to sell a utopian dream. People, whose content does not meet their standards or expectations, get put away, pulled apart, or taken down.

It becomes not so surprising that the videos on the "For You Page" all look the same, or at least very similar, since they follow the same process of treatment and elimination.

Reference can be made to a recent argument that erupted against the community rules and policies of the TikTok app to support this theory. It was involved in a controversy regarding their rulebook and their potential strategy of keeping less attractive people away from their famous "For You Page." It surfaced after documents, usually handed to their moderators, were leaked. They were posted on social networks to denounce the conditions of video selection accepted on TikTok, put forward or not by TikTok, and why.

These rules and reasons were simply shocking by their almost discriminatory claims and were massively criticized by all the media articles which had access to them. An interview with a TikTok representative took place shortly after, intended to interrogate them on these issues, but they mostly avoided the topic, assuring everyone that they were innocent.

Several terms deserved to be identified and analyzed to draw an inference on the intentions of TikTok and the true morals of the company. The document presented a very simple layout, with rules on the left and reasons on the right, implying the cause and effect of appearance traits that their creators could have or expose on their videos.

They seemed to determine, with terms archaic or obsolete, whether these videos were worthy of showing on their display page. These were arguments that we would expect to hear from someone living in the 1950s, when basic rights and decency were overshadowed by narrow-mindedness and the war that had just breathed its last. When body-shaming was more common, and yet, people were not as severely judged on their appearances as they are today.

Abnormal body shape.

Chubby.

Obese.

Too skinny.

Too many wrinkles.

Ugly facial looks.

Just to name a few.

These are indeed very pejorative and judgmental terms amongst many others that are used to describe creators and content unworthy of being presented or recommended to new users.

The Eradication of Humanity
By Social Media

For them, the "character" (a word which could almost mean, in this context, a certain shame or shock to the appearance of the performer) would then become the main focus of the video, instead of the content itself.

TikTok seems to be implying that seeing "obese" or "chubby" people, just to borrow their terms, would shock the viewers so much that they would not be able to focus on the message or the jokes that the person in question is trying to put through. That sounds like a petty excuse, as people come across all kinds of individuals in public areas like streets, stores, universities, or schools, and no one was ever bothered by it, shocked by it, or tried to make them leave because of their body proportions.

One thing is clear: only certain body types are worshipped on the Internet. They say beauty is in the eye of the beholder. Not so, according to app developers at TikTok.

The other terms – such as too ugly, fat, or skinny – are just as demeaning since the same way of thinking can be applied to them. No one ever shamed an old man for having wrinkles. It comes naturally with age, and no one can escape the passing of time. So why would this be a good reason to not put these people on display like all the others? TikTok's main goal is totally different from what they make it seem. In other words, less attractive people would diminish the appeal of the home page, and TikTok doesn't want that. It constantly needs to have more people visiting their app, and that works for them as an incentive. But that's only half the story!

Despite the body positivity movement flourishing on some social media apps, are their followers really supportive, or are they just looking for a group they can belong in?

The app also judges the decor in which a creator is surrounded by, and several criteria apply. Despite a creator's pleasant appearance and charming physique, he or she can still be rejected because the decor that they are shooting their video

114

with is "shabby" like "slums and rural fields," "dilapidated," "dirty," or "messy." Similar to what they think when they came up with the previously listed terms, TikTok describes this as the kind of environment that would look "less fancy and appealing" to new users of the platform. Once again, they are simply trying to relegate the backgrounds of all videos that supposedly could make the platform look less attractive and fun.

The additional problem here lies in the fact that a lot of people still live in poor conditions, but they are just as entitled as anyone else to post content on social media, be it for fun or to raise awareness of the conditions they have to live in every day. And because TikTok functions the way it does, their videos would never get any chance of making it to their main page because their decorations are "shabby" or "messy."

Without a doubt, TikTok's first concern lies within superficial criteria, which prove how shallow and cunning they really are. And, as if that wasn't enough, they were involved in a controversy that took on notable proportions regarding the processing and choice of content showcased on their platform.

Chapter Fourteen

Inclusive but Exclusive

If all that was mentioned so far regarded the physical appearance and demeanor of the people shown on videos, now, it will be on the silencing of minorities and "vulnerable" groups, such as those with physical or mental disabilities, marginalized ethnicities, LGBTQ+, etc. Those identified by these labels are often mocked, judged, or belittled by society because of their differences.

The Eradication of Humanity
By Social Media

This is a fact just as valid for people with darker skin, people who are attracted to the same sex, or even people suffering from mental disorders like depression or anxiety.

Discrimination can happen to anyone, anywhere. Despite civil rights movements gaining steam, such as those for racial justice via Black Lives Matter and Anti-Asian Hate education, people continue to be judged based on their appearances and abilities. This happens in real life, so, of course, we see it unfolding online as well. The digital world is the perfect place for biases to fester and grow. Hatred can be spewed from the convenience of a computer. Plus, there is the added anonymity. How convenient for racists and those who hold deep-rooted prejudices to be able to hide behind their keyboards?

Most of these victims cannot be identified by the naked eye, so how are they being targeted by TikTok's algorithm, and why are they supposed to be silenced when they have such a strong message to deliver? TikTok's answer to this is, once again, a vague and elusive one, just a temporary solution for the prevention of online harassment and bullying. As these people are "vulnerable," as they belong to groups of people who risk being targeted by the masses for being different, TikTok took them down from being included in mainstream videos. Punishing the victims seems to be their "perfect" solution for stopping the hate.

However, they had another option. One they chose not to take, one that maybe they never even considered. Despite all the mentions to its content moderators, TikTok never revealed that they were also in charge of the space dedicated to comments. Yet, it is obvious that this is where abusive people are going to spill the most hate. This is where the worst bullying phenomena occur on TikTok, so this is where they must intervene to reduce hateful remarks or gratuitous insults addressed to these communities.

Shouldn't they have tried to intervene there first?

The Eradication of Humanity
By Social Media

Shouldn't they have made certain words censored, or programmed alerts every time they are used so that moderators could judge for themselves whether the comment is hurtful or not?

Shouldn't they have assigned, or even employed, additional moderators to read comments, and remove all those which are harmful or offensive towards the creators to whom they are addressed?

Shouldn't they have assigned at least some sort of content moderation since they're so focused on their main page?

Or, are these precise and carefully-thought criteria only worth putting effort in to ensure new subscribers and the intact reputation of the app?

We must press for answers. Surely, there's a feature that allows them to disable the comment space on one or more videos altogether, but wouldn't this be just another temporary preventive measure, which could even cause the bullies to do worse as its tool is taken from them forcefully? Is this problem, though real, recurring, and extremely concerning, even a priority for them anymore? Or are they only throwing powder to make people believe they care and are trying their best, whether or not it's true?

People have always been prosecuted for being or believing in things differently from the major crowd. The Internet has given the most insecure and powerless bullies a way to reach others without divulging their identities. It's a way for them to hurt others without assuming or even facing the consequences of their blatant cruelty.

Is hiding the victims really the best way to protect the targets of bullies?

The Eradication of Humanity
By Social Media

Or is it only a way for TikTok to clear itself in case things go wrong?

Is it not a way for them to protect themselves from potential fallout instead of really trying to protect the minorities who they associate with weakness?

Racism on Twitch is a big problem. For example, users have claimed that, when a minority streams, there is almost always an influx of racist emojis. While an emoji on its own isn't racist, combinations are meant to communicate racist intentions. For instance, non-white faces paired with stereotypical foods. Out of context, this means nothing. A gun, a turban, or a chicken emoji is just that! An emoji. But gamers understand the not-so-subtle microaggressions when they appear in a chat featuring minority players. We *know* the language of social media. So, are we surprised that racists speak in these terms too?

Unfortunately, cyberbullying is also on the rise. What once was limited to the schoolyard is now a 24/7 reality for so many kids. Having the Internet at home means nobody is truly "unplugged" anymore. Before, if a child was the victim of bullying, it ended at school. Home was a safe space, a fortress that would-be attackers couldn't breach. Now, phones, computers, and devices make cyberbullying an insidiously easy option for those stalking their prey. Hateful messages are the norm, as is anonymous bullying. For kids who stand out, whether due to appearance, religion, gender orientation, or ability, nowhere is safe.

TikTok doesn't know how to handle problems related to minorities. This is the kind of matter that could tarnish the platform's image if it is managed poorly. Isn't it easier to just smother the flames before the fire spreads? By silencing minorities, they do keep them from getting submerged by the constant hate people are dumping on the Internet, but they also keep the world from knowing the truth, as hurtful or hateful as it may be.

The Eradication of Humanity
By Social Media

By no means is being a minority equivalent to being weak. They are discounted by a lot more people, which is why they are awkward and isolated. Because they don't always have someone to tell them that it is okay or even that they are not wrong. As it stands, it is only for selfish and foolish reasons that TikTok is keeping them away from their intended audience.

Maybe TikTok really wasn't created to be a place of meaning and sharing. Maybe it was always intended to be just a place where people could laugh, joke, and make silly challenges to amuse others. However, what the company behind its creation didn't see coming was that the freedom they give creators would always push them to tell their stories. And sadly, a lot of them end badly. These minorities (who still make up a small part of TikTok) have stories to tell and messages to deliver about life, pain, illnesses, or mental health.

They have advice to give and connections to make with people who went through the same experiences so they can try and survive together. And they are starting to get the support they need after huge events struck the web, like Black Lives Matter or even the American Elections. They started to notice that TikTok could also be a place of opening up and getting confessions off their chests.

Sadly, some people will stop at nothing to become famous. This includes abusing global catastrophes and health issues for their own personal gain. Take a look at the COVID-19 pandemic, for instance. Since the pandemic started in 2020, millions of people have used it to get popular on social media.

For some, it provided the perfect opportunity to express their political beliefs. Hell, even world leaders and politicians jumped on TikTok! They pointed fingers and blamed others while conveniently racking up hundreds of thousands of likes and gaining new followers. Those who identified as pro-vax or anti-vax did the same thing. For the modern-day attention seeker, COVID-19 was a hot button topic that propelled them into instant fame.

We wish it ended there, but we also see this in the videos of those who traveled to so-called "third world countries" on mission trips. They hopped on a plane, flew miles away from home, and landed in a foreign country with the will to help. Usually, this is driven by a good heart. We want to help build schools or dig wells for clean water. Of course, the desire to lessen the suffering of human beings is admirable.

What's concerning is the trend that follows, where volunteers record the whole trip on their phones, post videos of themselves, and garner attention from strangers on the Internet. The savior complex is so strong, as is the desire to be applauded online, that people don't see how problematic it is to record human pain without consent, just to be popular.

YouTube is the best example of this. Just search "mission trip" to get an idea of how bizarre the need for external validation is. Luckily, an American influencer, Hyram Yarbro, realized this. In a YouTube video titled, "I Was a Humanitarian...And I Regret It," he talks about this toxic culture. He admits that travel videos such as these trivialize the struggles of poor people, look down upon other countries, and use cultures for profit and popularity. Influencers who use humanitarian trips as a way to show off their goodhearted nature are, at best, misguided. At their worst, they are actively taking advantage of human suffering.

And even TikTok won't be able to entirely stifle this movement. People are woke now, interested in the world, and fighting for their rights. It isn't too much of a stretch to argue that, by limiting how minorities interact on the app, TikTok has gotten in the way of freedom of speech.

What will we do when everyone becomes so fearful of being cancelled or banned that they don't speak out at all? The last thing we need is a draconian 1984 Orwellian-style society. It's become way too easy for people to be silenced, like how celebrities who happen to say the wrong thing at the wrong time become obliterated. Ordinary people with different opinions shouldn't fear for their lives just because someone online disagreed with them or because their ideas angered somebody else. Social media should, in a perfect world, be an equalizing tool that gives everyone a voice. Instead, it seems to have become a weapon of mass destruction.

We're not supposed to talk about sensitive topics; otherwise, we won't be allowed on this platform. Nothing has ever been said in such straightforward words, but there is little to no evidence that TikTok hasn't said this either. People are starting to accept each other's differences, but will TikTok and social media ever do the same?

Is this the start of the end for people speaking freely on the Internet?

Or will they revolt when this growing tendency of shushing people trying to relay the truth stops going unnoticed?

Chapter Fifteen

The End of Humanity As We Know It

The argument we humbly put forth is that social media has the potential to end society as we know it. Look around—it's already happening. All across the globe, people are lonelier than ever. Our connections are suffering. Rather than asking

The Eradication of Humanity
By Social Media

out a new partner or attempting to forge new friendships, we stalk people online. Nobody calls anymore; we just message.

We brag about how enlightened we are, all while cyberbullying our enemies behind our computers. Even the way we shop has changed. Browse a store? Why bother when apps like TikTok exist where, with just a few short clicks, we can save ourselves the trip and order directly from websites that cater to our every desire. Society isn't changing. It has already changed. And not entirely for the better.

Social media is also ending society in other ways. Facebook is a uniquely good example. People use Facebook to brag about their relationships and break up with others. In a game of "Who is the happier wife?", women post endless photos of themselves with their husbands, smiling and kissing, even when they're fighting off-camera or when their partners aren't even real.

Friends compete for spots in their groups. We tag each other to make it look like we're all closer than we really are. Going through a bad breakup? Nowhere is better than Facebook to air dirty laundry. Or, if cheating is more our style, we can always send secret DMs we know our partners will never see. Take a look at the article called, "30 Complete Idiots Who Got Caught Cheating and Exposed on Facebook" if you don't believe that this is a huge problem. Remember, with social media, it's all about appearances.

Social media was intended to be a happy place. It was supposed to be a way to connect people, be it with family, friends, acquaintances, or even strangers. Many beautiful stories about people all around the world have come from the rise of social media. But there are some tragic and heartbreaking ones too. Social media was supposed to be a means to an end—a tool for people to use at their convenience, in the way they choose to. We need to ask ourselves some difficult questions.

The Eradication of Humanity
By Social Media

Why has it become a tool for manipulation, marketing, business, or communication in the hands of everyone?

How did it get so out of control that we don't even feel safe sharing our ideas or who we truly are?

Why are we not supposed to talk about the future anymore?

What will social media rob from us next?

The future of social media is as uncertain as its growth was when it first came into existence.

It can become Hell or Heaven, depending on what people try to do with it.

We must not allow social media to become more intrusive than it already has.

We cannot allow apps, like TikTok, to impede our freedom of speech simply because it fits whatever false utopian aesthetic the company finds suitable.

It must not be allowed to judge us before giving us the chance to introduce ourselves to the world properly.

TikTok must not be allowed to judge.

It must not be allowed to censor everything except what is disturbing, ethically questionable, or inadequate.

It must be compelled to accept and pursue change, which goes hand-in-hand with evolution.

People need to learn how to be authentic, how to be unique. Not from watching the same trends repeating endlessly or observing others sharing fake news or fake stories, but by trusting and accepting each other.

The Eradication of Humanity
By Social Media

TikTok and social media have turned into, "We must follow certain trends and behaviors, or else our lives are unimportant and don't matter."

Let's imagine a worst-case scenario. If social media evolved to become an obsessive and perplexing place where only a specific type of person can be idolized, would we consider dropping it? Would we stop using social media altogether, or would we abandon our morals and individual qualities to fold into a mold where everyone is similar? We know that our real lives aren't portrayed on social media. We are waking up, slowly, but surely. People are beginning to have problems with these dangers, concerned about having their futures decided for them as they should be! Let's hope it's not too late.

But before people completely turn against social media, we should start by correcting our own behaviors. People today are too distrustful of each other and preoccupied with nothing but themselves to see the misfortune of those around them. They only see their own paths, their own futures, and don't give importance to time and others. People today are too preoccupied with perfection and tend to forget that they, themselves, are imperfect also. Perhaps it is because they have been hurt too much.

Maybe they trusted others too much, and now, they don't dare to anymore.

Respect is earned, not given. The same can be said about trust. We, as users of social media, trusted the conglomerate to have our best interests at heart. We never dreamt that we would enter such a dark world of false promises and dangerous habits. Yet, here we are. We blindly follow the beautiful influencers who pander promises of happiness and fame, our real-life friendships deteriorating as we gain followers. The introduction of social media meant we had it all at our fingertips. Then why are we sadder than ever?

The Eradication of Humanity
By Social Media

Maybe it's all the pain we've pushed through and the people we've hurt to get to where we are.

Maybe it's fear that's holding us back.

Fear always keeps humans from doing something, even if they really want to.

It acts as a brake on our motivation and desire.

We are afraid of pain, so we avoid what can hurt us, and we are afraid of failure, so we seek to avoid opportunities that could offer us success.

We are afraid of being taken advantage of, so we avoid getting too close to others, and we are afraid of being demeaned, so we seek to dominate others.

And we are afraid of being alone, of disappointing, of no longer being loved.

We are afraid.

Just afraid.

But fear is powerful.

Fear can make people commit terrible acts.

All this to say, for these ordinary people like us, transited by fear without knowing it or admitting it, the Internet becomes a powerful motivator.

Why are we so desperate for Internet and TikTok fame?

Why do we see losing followers and fame as the end of the world?

The Eradication of Humanity
By Social Media

Why are we so desperate to establish a life and career online that we risk everything, including our lives?

The average person has five close friends, with many more acquaintances, such as colleagues, neighbors, distant relatives, etc. In the digital world though, those numbers increase into the hundreds. So, to the rational brain, it must seem ridiculous to get so upset when we lose followers. Yet, that's exactly what happens. We are so desperate for Internet fame that, when our followers choose to hit that "unfollow" button, it sends us spiraling. For some, it can even lead to depression. The anxiety around losing our popularity is all-consuming.

Social media users posting apology videos is now a commonplace occurrence, a desperate attempt to draw back their followers. We scream, rant, and cry, all in a last-ditch attempt to keep our fans. Some users have even gone so far as to risk their lives, posting dramatic videos where they threaten to kill themselves if they lose their followers. At the end of the day, we have to wonder if it's even worth it.

Logan Paul knows this better than anyone. His YouTube apology video called "So Sorry" has 59 million views. It also has 2.5 million downvotes.

In 2017, Logan Paul uploaded a controversial video to YouTube featuring the corpse of a man who committed suicide in the forests of Japan. On his channel, Paul wrote, "We Found a Dead Body in the Japanese Suicide Forest." Not only did Paul insensitively film the incident, but he also edited the video, uploaded it to his computer, and posted it on YouTube for all to see. No respect was shown to the victim or the man's family; no concern was given for the well-being of viewers. Paul literally filmed a suicide and seized the opportunity to mock a dead man, all for views.

The backlash was strong. Fans were disgusted. Logan risked everything for a minute of Internet fame. When it blew up in his face, guess what? Rather than learning from his mistakes, he, once again, took to social media in a vain attempt to win back his followers. Paul was so obsessed with notoriety that he sat with tear-soaked eyes and stared directly into the camera as he "promised to do better."

Is a YouTube star posting their crying fit online really doing better?

Or is it just another selfish shot at grabbing the limelight?

The Internet is a mysterious place where anything can happen. It bestows power onto people who lack the control they need. Everything they do comes from a wound they did not recover from. And somehow, they are inflicting it onto others for their own relief. They try to look for control elsewhere, without even thinking about the consequences of such heinous acts. Through an anonymous status, they express all kinds of venomous thoughts, wishing to slip by unnoticed and, by all means, unpunished.

Maybe if it were face-to-face, they wouldn't dare say a word. But behind a mask, every word comes to mind. Using it as an escape, trolls say all kinds of hurtful, injurious, and destructive words that were maybe said to them once a long time ago. They feel powerful. They feel like they have control over someone else's emotions. And they think that it must feel good.

These people don't blame themselves because they don't see its impact on the other person. They don't feel awful because the person who said it to them didn't either, and because they've hurt others in the same way, they think it's deserved and try to escape the responsibility that comes along with communication.

How are people expecting social media to not be manipulative and hateful when people manage to be even worse amongst themselves?

The Eradication of Humanity
By Social Media

Social media is, by its very nature, a manipulative beast. It works in insidious ways to convince us that without it, we can't be happy. Psychologists call this term FOMO – the fear of missing out. If everyone else is smiling and posting videos of themselves living their best lives online, and we aren't, then do we even matter? Are we not fun enough? Are our lives boring? Of course not. We all lead very individual and authentic existences. But these apps always manage to convince us that if we don't join the cult, we are the "weird" ones. We are the ones who don't belong. And so, we are peer pressured into participating.

It's a brainwashing tactic—an extremely successful one. There are claims that TikTok will purposely push a new user's first couple of videos so they get a higher number of likes. Suddenly, we feel seen; we feel important! And so, we keep posting. We keep doing whatever we must to be part of the game. We become brainwashed into believing that the more we play, the closer we will eventually get to winning. Very few of us ever wake up and realize that this game is rigged against us.

It bestows onto some people a paved way to fame that they still wish to shorten, even if it means using unreasonably sensitive topics they don't genuinely care about. Then they can show themselves as merciful, generous, and loving personalities who care about the well-being of the people involved. Many of them surfaced during the protests that minority populations have held in the United States to denounce the treatment and inequalities suffered by individuals with darker skin.

How many were sincerely concerned with how young girls and boys are told to hide when they cross the path of a white policeman? How many were honestly repulsed by how these children are raised to fear for their lives in a country that is supposed to be advanced and civilized? Though many considered it their duty to raise awareness amongst the most privileged, like a humanitarian mission allocated to them, others just took profit from the situation.

The Eradication of Humanity
By Social Media

It isn't just our friendships that suffer in our quest for fame. Family relationships also break down. All the time, people post their family drama on TikTok. Whether it's a divorce between parents, sibling rivalry, or other private matters, users of the app take this information and blast it from their speakers to get attention.

Some people have no shame at all, as seen in a disturbing trend involving grandparents. Examples are floating around TikTok right now of teens filming their ill grandparents, sometimes even on their deathbeds, and posting them online. All to get followers. All for the likes. They sacrifice an astonishingly intimate moment and warp it into something shallow and crude.

For example, let's go back in time. The year is 2006, the beginning of YouTube popularity. A user who goes by the name "lonelygirl15" posts a video she titled, "My Parents Suck…", during which she bemoans her parents for not allowing her to spend time with a boy named Daniel. At face value, this video (which has nearly 2 million views) is just like a retro episode of teenage drama. But the date is interesting. Even back as far as the early 2000s, we see social media being used as a platform to bash others for attention.

Whether "lonelygirl15" is acting or not is beside the point. What matters is that, even when social media was still a baby, people sacrificed others – including their families – to achieve fame.

Since then, the issue has only gotten worse. People kept chasing money or fame as if their lives depended on it. They tried to grasp it by all possible means, and sometimes, the desperation of not making it can be bewildering. Having outlived traumatic events or rough childhoods certainly made this feeling of belonging, need for attention, and thirst for success ever so present.

The Eradication of Humanity
By Social Media

We are ready to go to any lengths to obtain what we are looking for. In our eyes, the end justifies the means.

For example, a current trend is "flashbacks." With careful editing, teens and young adults pretend to go back in time to when they were little where something traumatic happened, like a neglectful parent or a mean teacher. The person then pretends to cry before being zoomed back to the "present day," where they explain how these terrible experiences affected them. In instances like this, TikTok almost serves as a public form of therapy. But weirdly, it's not for the betterment of the users. Once again, it's for the attention.

They play on emotions and trick people or incorporate references to both traumatic and sorrowful events to infiltrate their community. Pretending to have the same beliefs makes people more trusting and empathic, thinking they share a bond. One particular incident related to the use of trauma by inexperienced opportunists or ill-informed individuals does come to mind.

A term coined "trauma porn" refers to a fascination, sometimes borderline obsession, with other people's misfortune or pain. There are endless examples of this. One popular trend is domestic abuse. People (often girls) on TikTok use makeup to give themselves the appearance of an assault victim. Purple eyeshadow becomes bruises, red lipstick looks like blood, and sometimes, they rock and sway to imaginary punches. Their endgame? Supposedly to raise awareness about how spousal abuse has been on the rise during the global COVID-19 crisis. But how do real domestic abuse survivors who see these posts feel? Supported? Or do their experiences become trivialized, watered down into a fifteen-second attention grabber clip?

During August 2020, a debate arose on Twitter about what seemed to be a new trend on TikTok. It consisted of acting out an incarnation of Jewish people who died during the Holocaust, telling the stories of their dreadful and horrific experiences (often in the gas chambers) once they arrived in paradise.

Essentially, people on TikTok who had never experienced the horrors of war pretended to be Holocaust survivors. They dressed up in costumes and edited backgrounds to look like concentration camps or train stations. Girls acted out the parts of children and mothers while boys pretended to be the young men turned over to authorities.

The creators who carried this experience through to the end wore powder to imitate potential scars, bruises left by forced labor, and gas injuries. They dressed in ragged, dirty clothes or "uniforms" with the star of David. Each person gave a testimony of what these individuals had gone through, telling their story from a point of view never seen before. Although none of them took the subject lightly, it was not enough for Internet users to not feel insulted by the liberties the creators took regarding this matter.

Many individuals strongly criticized these practices on the part of ignorant people, having no culture about the real events of the Holocaust. Many lingered on the fact that these were mentions of traumatic events that could trigger reactions in people who are still suffering from them today. In general, people seemed to describe this practice with the words: offensive, hurtful, triggering.

It is undeniable that some of these individuals only surfed the trend in hopes of getting a large number of new subscribers. Many sought to showcase their acting skills, playing characters whose stories were touching and relatable. However, the general consensus is that they crossed the line this time around. One 17-year-old student, who preferred to remain anonymous and participated in this trend on TikTok, confidently claimed to have done so only to spread awareness and undeniable historical facts that must not be repeated but that young people need to be made aware of. She testified that she made this video only to educate others about the horrors that took place during the war.

Many in America are unaware of what happened during World War II on European soil. They, perhaps, felt less connected to these events as many had never seen museums, reconstructions, or the real institutions where these atrocities took place decades ago.

On the other hand, a 19-year-old Jewish woman named Briana sparked the debate on Twitter with a long thread about what these dishonorable practices and hurtful remarks could do to the survivors of these events. According to Diane Saltzman, director of survivor affairs at the US Holocaust Memorial Museum, it is a way to "trivialize history." The director invited young people to visit the museum to really experience these stories and learn the lessons accurately. Unfortunately, very few would really do so. This subject raises the question of cultural appropriation and transmission of ideas.

The fact that the creators do not belong to the ethnic group their videos portrayed drew comments that they had no right to make such statements. They claimed to understand what sickening experiences these victims went through, even though this was not part of their family culture. These appropriations can trigger hurtful memories for the people they were trying to protect, although some have acknowledged that this is still a commendable act on the part of the makers.

Cultural appropriation is another trending topic on TikTok. In light of BLM especially, conversations about what qualifies as cultural appropriation spring up daily. There are countless examples of videos arguing for and against dreadlocks on white individuals, for example. Some users claim this supports black culture, or their own, while others testify that they think it's wrong and only certain things can belong to specific groups. Either way, because it's happening on the Internet, insults always come out. Some people will even directly insult a culture,

The Eradication of Humanity
By Social Media

like when two non-Hawaiian girls danced the hula to make fun of it.

We won't debate who might be at fault in this controversy, but we can determine something. If, in the beginning, this trend was based on a pure desire to inform and confront young audiences with this reality in a way that museums do not have access to today, it has been misused and diverted by thousands of Internet users for much more dishonorable purposes. They have extracted all its humanity and good intentions from this concept, most of them surely without doing it on purpose, by simple ignorance and unconsciousness of youth. Once again, the desire for fame overruled common sense.

TikTok stayed silent throughout the whole controversy. At no point did one of their representatives take the mic to express how the company felt about the matter.

Did they not feel that they were responsible for what was filmed and shared on their platform?

Did they not feel like the videos infringed the moral purposes of the app's conditions of use?

Or they did, but their moderators did not suppress it or categorize it under hurtful content as they were supposed to?

Did they not feel like this recurring tendency needed to come to an end?

This isn't the first time social media giants have been tight-lipped in the face of controversy. When news broke of the Xinjiang internment camps targeting Uygur minorities in northwest China, Facebook, Twitter, Instagram, and TikTok were oddly quiet on the matter. Users around the globe publicly called out the social media platforms, many of which have news sections as part of their apps. Like it or not, many of us get our daily news updates from social media. Newspaper readership is declining. We turn to social media to be informed, and in return, we expect a certain degree of authenticity and responsibility on the part of the higher-ups running the show.

But when disturbing footage emerged about human rights being trampled in Xinjiang, TikTok, in particular, deleted users' videos, citing "inappropriate content." Like the Holocaust videos, these were immediately flagged. To avoid involvement or blame, social media platforms instituted a "no comment" policy.

Nonetheless, it is a fact that the app took down any related video, trying as much as possible to calm the waters. Today, none can be found on TikTok, and other creators have not posted videos regarding the issue to address this. The app made sure that they weren't responsible in any way. Given the emotionally delicate situation, an uncomfortable or indecisive speech would only have aggravated the triggered victims, even more so if they took the issue too lightly. So, somehow, it was the right choice for them to stay silent.

And whilst sensitive issues like these have been swept under the rug, TikTok continues to ask their moderators to suppress what they judge as "unfavorable" content under their own criteria, which seemed to have missed the videos mentioned earlier. It makes you wonder what these criteria might even be about...

TikTok failed to delete the offensive survivor videos when released, but it has not failed to suppress and erase thousands of others for far less of an inconvenience. It is not the first, nor the last time, that TikTok's moderators, with their rulebook in hand, have deleted videos or accounts because their content was deemed "unfavorable" from their perspective.

When faced with issues regarding the content young teenagers could have access to, TikTok claimed to adopt a zero-tolerance policy, with the main objective of protecting minors, for example, closely monitoring how teens share content with nudity, dangerous, or otherwise risky behavior such as drugs, alcohol, etc.

TikTok warned us that it would be ruthless towards the content reported by its moderation rules, and its systems would identify suspicious forms or behaviors and automatically detect any material that may violate its Community Rules. The app would seek, for the sake of transparency (and surely to avoid potential lawsuits), to remove as many of the videos at risk as possible in order to avoid incidents later on.

If you're determined, there is always a way to bend the rules. Cropping or blurring videos so that only some body parts are visible is one way. Since users know they can't explicitly post nudity, there is a trend where they will post a clip of themselves looking "nerdy," followed by a musical transition. In the split-second change, they plug in a lightning-fast image of themselves in underwear, or for men, shirtless.

These "thirst trap" videos technically aren't encouraged by TikTok, but because they don't explicitly violate guidelines, they are allowed. If you want to judge for yourself, just search #sexysilhouettechallenge.

Anyway, that was TikTok's goal. But this policy is as commendable as it is frightening. TikTok has admitted, along with these claims, that it has already deleted 49 million videos from its platform. What is worrisome is not the excessive number, but rather the fact that some these videos had (by logical deduction) stayed online while maybe going against their policies, and the fact that other videos that were removed may not display the dangerous or sensitive content they thought they did. The platform is overflowing with new videos, with hundreds uploaded every hour. How do they expect to control and moderate each and every single one of them thoroughly?

Well, they don't. They expect their system to find most of the sensitive content, and their moderators take charge of the rest.

The Eradication of Humanity
By Social Media

They do it haphazardly. TikTok's algorithm, as imperfect as it is, doesn't only detect videos that are reprehensible and should truly be dismissed. It can also misinterpret the videos it analyzes and tag them as potentially dangerous. Despite the hard work TikTok users put into creating videos, all it takes is attracting the unwanted attention of the algorithm to block, erase, or shut down an account.

Even if these are nothing more than popular assumptions thrown around on the Internet, they are the most serious and believable. And since TikTok does not know the exact reasons for which the system detection software identifies videos as "sensitive," it sometimes gives baseless and useless pretexts to deleting them. Better safe than sorry, right?

Ultimately, it's like a case of the boy who cried wolf. Videos that violate community standards squeeze past the detectors while harmless ones get deleted. Many creators on TikTok have reported deletions of their videos in an abusive and unfair way. They argue that their videos were not, in any way, against the TikTok Community Rules, and the strangest fact is that everybody seems to ignore their exact content and outline. The algorithm might be a helpful tool, but it's not perfect.

TikTokers insist on having reproduced the exact same challenge or concept as everyone else, but some end up being victims to the algorithm's unfairness. Often, these seemingly unreasonably targeted individuals claim that their videos are being deleted, and when they seek to appeal this unilateral decision, their messages and complaints remain unanswered. And given the time invested by many of them in their videos, it is understandable that they cry foul when their content is forcibly removed from the platform.

As social media users, our loyalty is up for grabs. If an app fails to adapt to the needs of its users, eventually, it will become extinct. For example, Facebook is dying. Sure, the social media giant is rolling out new features constantly as it tries to adapt to a younger crowd. But Facebook's algorithms and goals are out of sync with the current users.

Frustration seems to be the main component of the still-growing dissatisfaction in the hearts of social media users and, in particular, TikTok's users. It is agonizing for them to be treated differently and never understand why. Some people have already resigned themselves to the sad reality of the algorithm's random accusations. Most people, far from agreeing with their assumptions, contest their decision by posting the content multiple times with slight changes, trying to understand which part of it was problematic and hoping that, this time, it will stick around. In our pursuit of attention and fame, we dedicate even more time, energy, and thought into playing detective.

However, TikTok should know by now that nothing stays hidden forever. Secrets breed mistrust, and it is not easily recovered. If creators lose their trust in a platform's proactiveness and the future it holds in store for them, there is no way around the decisive end of its supremacy. People don't like being cheated or lied to, nor do they react well to tricks and manipulations. They would react better to a good-willed confession rather than an excuse for having hidden the truth for so long. Unless TikTok's criteria and Community Rules are proved to be cruel or discriminative, there is no apparent reason to keep them under wraps for so long.

As the people keeping this app alive, we deserve transparency.

We deserve the truth.

Chapter Sixteen

TikTok's Diversity, For Better and For Worse

Without a doubt, we can file this app under the following designation: Dark and Mysterious TikTok. It's another reality that has recently surfaced, thanks to Internet users bringing this strange phenomenon to light. It has spread like wildfire, with many forced to acknowledge its existence even if they don't want to.

Only by researching and typing specific hashtags, can one gain access to the darker side of the app. For the sake of research or pure misplaced curiosity, some people have ventured to the other side only to find gory, creepy, disturbed, pedophilic, or violent videos. These types of content should have long been deleted and moderated, but they somehow still manage to escape the grasp of TikTok's algorithm. Does TikTok even know that these videos exist? Is the app willfully blind? If yes, why are they letting them go unchecked?

Two facts should be dealt with upfront. First, if there was no audience to view these unhealthy or disturbing videos, they would never have been published, or at least, not in such large numbers. The human instinct does not push us to produce in vain, to waste time or energy for a result that will prove to be disappointing or uninteresting. There is an audience for these videos, whether out of misplaced curiosity or motivated by an unhealthy admiration for traumatic content. Like moths to the flame, we can't resist.

Earlier, we briefly mentioned trolls. Even at their worst, they help our accounts grow. We obsess over them and reply to their nasty bait. Trolls serve a purpose in pushing us to our limit in terms of engaging in unsafe behavior. If they call us "boring," we become extreme. If they say we're "ugly," we physically mutilate our bodies to become #beautifulbabes. They make us angry, insult the brands we love and our sense of style, or anything at all, so long as it provokes a knee-jerk reaction. They're trolls, after all—they feed off our emotions.

For instance, look at the case of Amanda Todd, a fifteen-year-old girl who committed suicide. After being blackmailed for showing pictures of her breasts on the Internet, Todd became a victim of relentless trolling and bullying from her peers. Classmates at her school created a Facebook page just to make fun of her. Trolls wrote insensitive comments about her experience with anxiety, depression, prior suicide attempts, and passed judgments on her moral character.

Finally, she had enough. Tragically, Amanda Todd hung herself. For kids like her, trolls aren't just annoying jerks with too much time on their hands. They are real threats. Amanda Todd didn't engage in silly stunts or dares for attention, but haters participated in creating dangerous content that ultimately took her life.

If everyone else jumped off a bridge, would we too? It's the age-old question. Without an audience, we probably wouldn't do half of the stupid things we do for attention. Viewers, and yes, even our haters, fuel content creators into risking their lives and creating dangerous material. We see it in the challenges that go viral. Also, in the way we respond to our haters. They push us, and we react by going to unsafe places, trying dangerous activities, or even going so far as to inject or ingest substances.

Some individuals make this type of content regardless of the platform they are on. Whether it's to satisfy a need for fame (like others but by taking a darker path) or for psychological needs, there will, unfortunately, always be a detour from the primary intentions of online social applications. These psychedelic posts, which escape the comprehension of many people, including their creators, interest us more than we would like to admit. This seems to awaken an instinct of voyeurism that humans infrequently confront, leading to a disproportionate general interest.

In essence, we are all like sheep. Once a celebrity or influencer promotes something for people to try, like the Benadryl challenge, people blindly follow despite the dangers. When popular influencers started talking about how fun the #nutmeg challenge was, swarms of teens quickly jumped on the bandwagon. In an effort to get high, they injected large

142

amounts of nutmeg mixed with water into themselves, causing seizures in at least one case.

The fact that people even feel the need to post this kind of content is upsetting, if not revolting. Maybe they were looking for a slightly less blinding atmosphere in which to perform, using their dark sense of humor, and talk about their ambitions. Or perhaps, these obsessive tendencies have only decided to come forward after being given a stage of their own. If only the answer was so simple and straightforward.

Two types of content stand out in this context. The first one is none other than a kind of cult, which seems to have been born on this emerged side of the platform. If the term seems a bit exaggerated, the reality remains that people have gathered for a new type of video. It involves an, "Are you coming to the tree?" banner, and many individuals seem to recognize themselves in the aesthetics and the message it seems to convey. Perhaps further research will help us understand whether this is just a trend that's part of a tasteless joke, or a small movement among deviant people.

Most of these creators share distorted, saturated videos, full of visual glitches and skinny faces lined with a special filter, against a background sound that seems to come from a horror video game with a distorted voice formulating a kind of invitation. The comment space is even more chaotic than the videos themselves. There is a clever mix of bizarre writings that are impossible to read, messages saturated with emojis (mostly trees and knives), and finally, many invitations to become one of the Tree's people . . . whatever that means.

Following the same trend, they give sacrifices to trees (like hair, for instance) while using references for satanic cults and witchcraft. It's frightening. And that's why we love it. For the same reason we watch horror movies, some of us are drawn to the more macabre side of TikTok.

The Eradication of Humanity
By Social Media

It is possible to find other types of videos under these same hashtags: papier-mâché dolls hanging and doing strange dances, dolls being stabbed with knives, people filmed spraying themselves with a brownish liquid in a shower, eating little baby figurines out of a bowl like cereal, and people talking about avenging trees, among others.

As much as we would like to excuse these particular practices as plain dark humor, it remains that they are weird, creepy, and potentially dangerous. Let's just hope they do not grow even more just to attract viewers...

The second one is none other than scary staged videos; users set up a stage as realistically as possible, then tell a creepy story from the point of view of a main character. Many people enjoy this thrilling content, and its creators are becoming more and more original.

Some accounts have become known for their original concepts. A guard in charge of security of a necropolis where tombs are stored filmed strange phenomena that occurred in his workplace, mainly at night. A child's voice was sometimes heard in the distance, and the man would eventually investigate to find the source.

Another man staged in a sandwich shop (his workplace) and proclaimed that he saw strange phenomena, which could almost be called "manifestations of spirits" that occurred daily around him. Lamps swinging on their own, strange noises, objects falling down without anyone touching them, or lights that go out and come back on again from a distance. Paranormal activity? Or simply a creator hoping to gain new followers? As the audience, it's left for us to decide.

People faking their own deaths, or the deaths of others, for attention is not a new concept. What *is* new is the degree of clout these garner in the modern age. Clearly, such antics are popular! As time goes on, the boundaries between what is just good, silly fun and what is unacceptable get blurrier and blurrier.

One person pushed the story even further, saying that he found a chest or box containing patient labels and strange documents in a hidden space in his attic. They supposedly came from a psychiatric hospital, so he began researching the patients' names.

Many others are trying to create this kind of content, some of them finding it very entertaining, which are entirely staged by its creators without the slightest hint of pretentiousness and, above all, without ever really creating terror or disgust in the face of explicit scenes. It doesn't mean that this type of material is not scary or terrifying, or even that, among the staged fake videos, there aren't actually real ones trying to alarm people and warn them of danger...

We will do anything for that perfect photo. Nowhere is this exemplified better than on Instagram, which can also promote dangerous behavior, all for the perfect picture. One famous example happened in Yosemite National Park. Moorthy and Viswanath ran an Instagram page dedicated to photographing beautiful destinations, outdoor adventure, and world travel. At the time of their deaths, they had over twenty-two thousand followers, but all was lost in a matter of seconds. While taking a selfie, they both fell 800 feet over the edge of a cliff.

This isn't just a one-time crazy example.

In New Zealand, Rachael Louise De Jong drowned in the Waikato River while posing for a selfie when the dam waters rose.

In Canada, three people died at Shannon Falls, a popular waterfall known for its beauty and dangerous terrain. Megan Scraper got too close to the edge when she slipped on the rocks.

The Eradication of Humanity
By Social Media

Her two companions tried to save her but also lost their lives in the 335-meter-tall falls.

In China, a man was killed after trying to take a selfie with a walrus at a zoo.

In Spain, a spectator left the safe zone during a running of the bulls event because he wanted a selfie in front of the magnificent animals. Instead, he was gored to death.

The problem is so bad that some tourist hotspots now have "no selfie" signs posted. However, this isn't enough to dissuade all the attention-hungry influencers. We will do anything for the perfect photo, including risking and sacrificing our lives.

Let's turn away from selfies and look further outwards for a moment. Among the diversified recreational videos, problematic scandals have arisen from the unchecked content or the app's excessive popularity that incites people to use it to broadcast unspeakable acts.

One of the few involved another popular app called "Randonautica," which has grabbed the headlines, thanks to its massive following and exposure on TikTok. Thanks to its worldwide popularity, the application now has a real impact on the success or failure of certain businesses, and if these go viral for one reason or another, its popularity will only skyrocket. The particular concept of Randonautica, which seems quite enigmatic, was meant to push people into going out more often, discovering local or regional peculiarities with a specific goal in mind.

We bring up this topic because it can also be extremely dangerous. Apps like Randonautica encourage us to push our comfort levels to the point of stupidity. Encouraging risky actions, like hiking to obscure locations deep in the woods, up mountainsides with no outdoor gear, or near waterways that might not be monitored, are all reasons why Randonautica users should be careful.

So, how does it work? The website generates a randomized set of GPS coordinates that should lead users to beautiful but hidden landscapes or previously surprise setups left by others. These are places where people are meant to discover something they are later invited to share on the app's forum. Some have encountered spooky coincidences, while others find borderline dangerous setups, but none as traumatic and nauseating as this one.

Consider the following case. This app led a group of teenagers to a local beach. After looking around for a bit, they found a suitcase at the exact spot they were supposed to examine. The atmosphere, which had been full of laughter and adventurous expectations, grew cold as they smelled something putrid and unidentifiable. Some of them probably hypothesized that there was decaying food inside, but it was something else entirely. They gathered the courage to open the suitcase, and even though they could not say what exactly was inside the black garbage bag, they knew they had to call the police.

Once the cops arrived on the scene, the police revealed the chilling truth behind the suitcase: the application had led them to the location of a tool that a murderer had used to hide the body parts of an individual he'd killed. These teens signed up for an adventure. Instead, what they got was accidental involvement in a murder investigation. Oops.

This case is concerning for multiple reasons. Searches like this one are dangerous. *Anyone* can propose coordinates on the Randonautica site that can lead random people to the same general area. We don't know who has been there or what objects they left behind. Or scarier still, who might be lurking there when we arrive!

The Eradication of Humanity
By Social Media

Kidnappers and rapists aren't ignorant to social media either. Just as killers have used apps like TikTok to their advantage when hiding a corpse, so do other criminals. After the film "365 Days" became a hit on Netflix, TikTok clips began trending, where people would pretend to either be sexy kidnappers or beautiful hostages. Kidnapping and rape became glorified. Those with romantic kidnapper fantasies were served with the content of their dreams.

Rather than condemning these vile behaviors, TikTok feeds into such illusions, promoting imaginary rape and kidnapping scenarios.

What real-life consequences can normalizing these behaviors have?

A similar case of using the Internet for harmful purposes has arisen, this time, directly on TikTok, which is said to be linked to the Italian mafia. Some claim the mafia seeks to recruit new candidates and are communicating about organized crime through specific hashtags. The video that launched this trend was filmed in an Italian high-security prison. A man, whose identity is not known, filmed a TikTok exposing the living conditions inside. The Italians then talked a lot about them, launching a real trend that other Mafiosi would later put into practice.

The latter thus exposes their daily practices: weapons, drugs, crimes. To prove their supremacy, increase their influence by claiming higher positions, and at the same time, lure in young people, these Mafiosi will stop at nothing. And it is impossible to say what kind of life these young people will lead afterwards, led by admiration and intimidation, subjected to obedience by demonstrations of violence. All of this to be like them, to get their influence, their power, and their money. But not many official sources have effectively researched this situation.

Other scandals, less related to organized crime or murder, have also emerged. And the targets are none other than children or young adolescents. As mentioned before, many kids under the recommended age of 13 still roam around the app, sometimes even posting content themselves. We're not discussing whether or not 13 is old enough to use social media (it is the minimum age for registration), but that these children must be protected. TikTok, which claims to do its best to delete the accounts of these creators who violate their terms of use, also puts the responsibility back on the parents, who must supervise their children.

This, of course, raises the question: are children mature enough to expose themselves and to be exposed on social networks? Without an answer to this question, it's obvious that dangers remain, and they are likely to be confronted with them.

Pedophilia is the first concern. Indeed, a growing presence of perverts on TikTok has been reported, which shouldn't be shocking. They see the app as an opportunity to feed on their guilty pleasures. These individuals focus on following young girls, liking "sexy" videos or, even worse, asking for inappropriate material (such as nude photos) through the comments. How can the app even fight back? It has no way of checking a person's identity. When registering, there is no need to provide a valid name, age, gender, or even address.

How do we catch a predator if we don't even know they exist?

Stalkers are also a concern. On Facebook, we are encouraged to check in with our contact list and visit pages to see what our friends are up to. But at what point does this become stalking? We've all used social media to investigate someone secretly. We want to see who they are, after all, before committing to getting to know them better. In the age of social media, we don't go into coffee shops anymore; instead, we creep.

The Eradication of Humanity
By Social Media

Once or twice is normal, but when it becomes a daily habit? Well, we are entering stalker territory.

Okay, so we found someone we like. Maybe it's a potential boyfriend or a long-lost great-aunt. If we aren't already friends, then the information we can see is limited. So, what do we do? We add them. Because Facebook is temporal, meaning posts are shared live and get old in "real-time," it actually promotes active stalker behavior. We feel like we constantly need to be checking in on people's morning, noon, and night, just in case we missed something important they shared while we're offline.

If you feel sneaky or slimy while doing this, that's good. Skulking around somebody's online persona isn't natural. We want to connect, but instead, we are reduced to spying.

In this imaginary scenario, let's say we get blocked. The person we are stalking gets wise and doesn't like our lurking. No problem, because we can still make a phantom account to follow them or go through a mutual friend. The same goes for Instagram.

For example, in California, Jonathan Ward was charged with stalking. He broke into a thirteen-year-old girl's house after tracking her activity on Instagram. Luckily, the police arrived before anyone got hurt, but Ward was naked when he was arrested. His case got a lot of notoriety and raised the question: if it was that easy for a stalker to get inside, how easy would it be for others to do the same?

Or worse?

How can we expect TikTok, or any social media for that matter, to fight an invisible enemy who stays hidden in the shadows, behind a fake profile no one can see through? TikTok has been frequently designated as an app for narcissists, for people whose lives revolve around their looks or their appearances, nothing else. But now, there is a steadily growing tendency for people to objectify and sexualize young women and men for their pleasure or entertainment.

Children and young teenagers are increasingly reproducing adult behaviors, and the trivialization of this hyper-sexualization is both disturbing and sad to witness. Adolescents want to grow up faster, become like the beautiful women they admire faster. TikTok appears concerned with the protection of children, but it's not obvious to its users what the app is doing towards eradicating these kinds of threats on a supposedly family-user-friendly app…

What could have been a good solution to this emerging inquiry, but wasn't suggested by TikTok until now, was the creation of an independent version of the app (like a version of TikTok more suitable for kids) with children at its core and content meant specifically for them. Instead of finding invisible, ineffective, and meaningless ways to protect them (that sadly, pedophiles or ill-intended people will always manage to bypass), maybe creating a safe place for them would be better suited.

Everything is not all doom and gloom, however! We do have ideas on how to make the app safer. For example, the conditions of registration would have to be stricter than the original app. For the security and children's peace of mind, that should not be a heavy price to pay. Children would then stop being targets of unhealthy relationships and would only view adequate content created by other children. But would TikTok even consider such a solution, however peaceful it may seem at first sight?

And last, but not least, the most depressing event that turned most users' stomachs upside down was the tragic suicide video that made the news on August 31, 2020. It was first posted on Facebook by Ronnie McNutt, who took his own life during a live stream by gunshot, but then it became viral. The video was available and up on Facebook for more than two and a half hours until the network finally decided to erase it, as well as all the excerpts, photos, or discussions that could still circulate around the Internet. Many users criticized and described the giant's intervention as "too late," "irresponsible," and "disrespectful of the human life that had just been lost." Apparently, Facebook's tech experts struggled to keep the video's virality under control, which led to their delayed intervention.

Unfortunately, many of the users present on the platform that day witnessed this scene, and out of curiosity, as gruesome as it was unhealthy, many of those who were unable to watch the video tried to find it as soon as the news reached them. This sad will and psychological instinct to want to face death, to want to admire it with one's own eyes, is certainly considered normal and understandable by some scientists, but it is no less disturbing. Some took advantage of these two hours to share the video en masse on different networks, even the least reputable and secure ones.

But it is definitely on TikTok that the virality increased, in a tragic and vicious way, as it was massively relayed by reckless and wicked individuals, devoid of common sense and life skills. Some creators have included excerpts from the video, especially from the moment of the final *bang*, and embedded them in innocent recordings of kittens and other such content to hide it while making it accessible to other users of the platform.

And herein lies the major problem. As obscure as it was maniacal, this led many people to view these tragic and gloomy scenes without their consent. Many Internet users sought to prevent this, sharing massive alert messages on all networks to reach as many people as possible. And others sought to denounce those who had reproduced the original video, at the same time, attacking all those cruelly tactless who claimed to want to get their hands on the original video to watch it.

All that can be said is that after considering every aspect, TikTok has attained the rank of a social media giant, and its growth doesn't seem to be slowing down anytime soon. But what has become crystal clear is that the app is at the heart of many scandals and controversies.

Many users are concerned about the future use of the application, which could continue being misused for harmful purposes. It is, in general, surrounded by mysteries, secrets, and mischievous plots, which all seem to converge into feeding people an idealized version of reality and making them grow dependent on the platform.

No social media network has ever been created or optimized for the sake of its users.

As old social media trends die, new ones will arise to take their place. In this book, we examined how TikTok, Facebook, Instagram, YouTube, and Twitch have all revolutionized how people interact with one another. The Internet brought about much good, but our lives and futures have unquestionably changed for the worse because of social media. Yes, the solution is as easy as going offline or uninstalling the app. But how many of us are willing to make that sacrifice? What will happen if we can't change the course of the dark path we are on?

Rather than helping us, social media has taken advantage of our psychological and social needs. It aims to reach goals that are in direct conflict with our own. TikTok is ultimately just a means to an end. And this last case gave a clear glimpse of who really represents a problem in this equation: human beings or new technologies, such as the Internet? The analysis is quick to make.

People will do anything for fame and wealth.

Someday, it will destroy us.

The Eradication of Humanity
By Social Media

The Eradication of Humanity
By Social Media

The Eradication of Humanity
By Social Media

www.ingramcontent.com/pod-product-compliance
Lightning Source LLC
LaVergne TN
LVHW042336060326
832902LV00006B/201